THINK BIG
start small

How to **Differentiate Instruction**
in a **Brain-Friendly Classroom**

Gayle
GREGORY

Martha
KAUFELDT

W9-BON-495

Solution Tree | Press

a division of

Solution Tree

555 North Morton Street
Bloomington, IN 47404

800.733.6786 (toll free) / 812.336.7700
FAX: 812.336.7790

email: info@solution-tree.com
solution-tree.com

Visit **go.solution-tree.com/instruction** to download the reproducibles and access live links to the websites in this book.

Printed in the United States of America

15   4 5

Library of Congress Cataloging-in-Publication Data

Gregory, Gayle.

  Think big, start small : how to differentiate instruction in a brain-friendly classroom / Gayle Gregory, Martha Kaufeldt.

    p. cm.

  Includes bibliographical references and index.

  ISBN 978-1-935543-06-0 (perfect bound) -- ISBN 978-1-935543-07-7 (library edition) 1. Individualized instruction. 2. Cognitive styles in children. 3. Mixed ability grouping in education. 4. Learning, Psychology of. 5. Brain. 6. Classroom environment. I. Kaufeldt, Martha, 1954- II. Title.

  LB1031.G748 2012

  370.15'23--dc23

                    2011030375

Solution Tree
Jeffrey C. Jones, CEO & President

Solution Tree Press
President: Douglas M. Rife
Publisher: Robert D. Clouse
Vice President of Production: Gretchen Knapp
Managing Production Editor: Caroline Wise
Senior Production Editor: Lesley Bolton
Proofreader: Elisabeth Abrams
Text and Cover Designer: Amy Shock

Acknowledgments

Solution Tree Press would like to thank the following reviewers:

John Almarode
Assistant Professor, Department of Early, Elementary, and Reading Education
James Madison University
Harrisonburg, Virginia

George Rod Larsen
Science Department Chair
West Orange High School
Winter Garden, Florida

Katie Martin
3rd–5th Grade Reading Teacher
Elizabeth Cady Stanton Elementary School
Seneca Falls, New York

Jerald Schenck
4th Grade Teacher
Wrightsville Elementary School
Wrightsville, Pennsylvania

Marilee Sprenger
Educational Consultant
Peoria, Illinois

Visit **go.solution-tree.com/instruction** to download the reproducibles and access live links to the websites in this book.

Table of Contents

3 Engaging, Exciting, and Energizing the Learner 49

4 Exploring the Learning 67

5 Extending and Expanding Learning for Every Student 91

About the Authors

Gayle Gregory has been a teacher in elementary, middle, and secondary schools; community colleges; and universities. She has had extensive districtwide experience as a curriculum consultant and staff development coordinator. Gayle was principal and course director at York University for the Faculty of Education and taught in the teacher education program. Gayle's focus and interests are in the field of mind, brain, and education, incorporating neuroscience and cognitive and educational psychology. Her areas of expertise include brain-compatible learning, block scheduling, emotional intelligence, instructional and assessment practices, differentiated instructional strategies, collaborative learning, presentation skills, renewal of secondary schools, enhancing teacher quality, coaching and mentoring, managing change, and building professional learning communities.

Her many books and videos focus on quality instruction, assessment, and collaboration for learning for all ages, incorporating what we are learning from all the sciences as well as pursuing the art of teaching.

Gayle is committed to lifelong learning and professional growth for herself and others. To learn more about Gayle's work, visit www.gaylehgregory.com.

Martha Kaufeldt began her teaching career in 1977. For twenty-three years, she taught elementary, middle, and high school. She began her research of brain-compatible teaching and learning strategies while working with several school districts to develop gifted, talented, and extended-learning programs. She served as program director, trainer, and coach for the Bay Area Middle Schools Project for five years. Martha returned to the middle school classroom and worked on an interdisciplinary teaching team. As a new challenge, Martha then worked for four years as the restructuring coordinator and lead teacher at an alternative K–6 public elementary school in Santa Cruz, California. This unique program emphasized brain-compatible teaching strategies, differentiated instruction, multiage classes, authentic assessment, parent participation, and conflict resolution strategies.

When her schedule allows it, Martha continues to rotate back into the classroom as a long-term substitute or guest teacher to help build up her "tackle box of strategies." Martha is a popular presenter at conferences and conducts workshops and trainings internationally.

Martha has a master's degree in human behavior and development. Her previous books include *Begin With the Brain: Orchestrating the Learner-Centered Classroom* and *Teachers, Change Your Bait! Brain-Compatible Differentiated Instruction*. To learn more about Martha's work, visit www.beginwiththebrain.com.

To book Gayle Gregory or Martha Kaufeldt for professional development, contact pd@solution-tree.com.

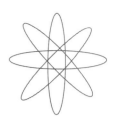

Introduction

Differentiation is neither revolutionary nor something extra. It is simply teaching mindfully and with the intent to support the success of each human being for whom we accept professional responsibility.

—*David A. Sousa and Carol Ann Tomlinson*

"What *is* this new buzzword *differentiated instruction*?" This question was posed to one of us recently. The reply was simple. New? Hardly. Great teachers have been differentiating instruction for hundreds of years—they know their curriculum, see who shows up, and design learning experiences that respond to students' needs/readiness, interests, preferences, and learning profiles. Then if some students get it quickly and at a deeper level, these teachers challenge them. If others don't get it the way it is taught, they reach into their toolkits and try another approach.

Differentiation is the core of the art and science of teaching. While some teachers differentiate intuitively, others need guidance, encouragement, and a tackle box of ideas. However, even when equipped with a large repertoire of strategies, if the teacher doesn't have a basic understanding of how the human brain grows, develops, and learns, he or she may not be effective in the classroom. Using clever strategies in a "brain-antagonistic" environment often fails.

Understanding some brain basics from neuroscience research on learning, attention, memory, emotions, and stress can serve as a solid foundation for designing classroom environments, curricula, and instructional strategies. While some may think that educational neuroscience is being applied prematurely in classroom practice and is, perhaps, a bridge too far, many believe that as educators understand more about how brains work best, they will see natural applications within the learning process.

What We Know About Learning

As young children, both of us had wonderful families who stimulated all our senses in enriched, supportive, and stable environments. We were encouraged to explore and discover things that interested and motivated us without fear of failure or repercussions.

Our early years at school were full of more opportunities to develop socially and emotionally and learn like sponges with engaging teachers in risk-free environments. We each developed passions for music, drama, and creativity. We appreciated great teachers who engaged us and opened new worlds with their ability to make their subjects come alive with interesting and creative learning processes and strategies that challenged us and were appropriate to our skill and knowledge capacities. We were encouraged to create projects and models to demonstrate our understanding and make sense of new concepts, skills, and information. We experienced variety and choices that gave us some autonomy to engage in topics and materials that were of interest to us and relevant to our lives. Our teachers were using brain-compatible strategies decades before the "decade of the brain." Intuitively, these clever educators recognized that people learn differently, that engaging the senses mattered, and that learners needed a sense of control over their own learning.

As teachers ourselves, we went through basic training and lesson planning but also wanted to engage students, knowing that they were all wired differently from their genetic and environmental backgrounds. We wanted learning to be exciting and interesting as we ourselves didn't want to be bored every day doing the same thing. It was a process of trial and error to discover what connected with students and captured their attention and minds.

When the emerging field of educational neuroscience presented itself to us in the 1980s, we were curious, eager learners who wanted to know all we could about the brains of our students. Much of what we learned validated what we were doing in classrooms and encouraged us to try other techniques to engage our students and enhance their learning and memory. We were ready to use action research to discover and understand what worked for our special education, gifted, and general education students. We also realized that the instructional strategies that increased student percentile gains got on the best-dressed list because they supported how the brain learns best. The following statement from two of our mentors makes good sense:

> As we gain a greater understanding of how the human brain learns, we may discover ways to better meet the needs of our increasingly diverse student population. Sometimes, students are attempting to learn in environments that are designed to help but inadvertently hinder their efforts. By looking for ways to differentiate instruction and change some of our assessment approaches, we may be able to help more students achieve their full potential. (Sousa & Tomlinson, 2011, p. 5)

Action research has been going on since the 1990s in many classrooms. Some neuro-myths like "drinking more water or eating chocolate helps the brain learn better" were initially promoted by some teachers who were eager to use what they believed were brain-based techniques. However, such neuromyths are just that—myths. According to Dénes Szücs and Usha Goswami (2007):

> There is a fundamental difference between doing educational neuroscience and using neuroscience research results to inform education. While current neuroscience research results do not translate into direct classroom applications, educational neuroscience can expand our knowledge about learning. (p. 114)

Mind, brain, and education (MBE) is a growing field that is incorporating neuroscience and cognitive and educational psychology. Research on gender differences, learning preferences, and students' thoughts and behaviors should be considered when designing an environment that maximizes learning. We will discuss at least seven well-substantiated brain principles (see chapter 1) that will influence classroom practice.

Differentiation in a Brain-Friendly Classroom

Busy teachers are often overwhelmed with the task at hand: Take twenty-five plus students from various backgrounds on a successful learning journey for 180 days. Make sure they each hit these benchmarks by spring, and be sure to integrate the use of cutting-edge technology into the lessons. Although the instructional budget has been cut by 50 percent and there will be no field trips this year, inspire your students to become lifelong learners . . . and so on. This is a common scenario, not the exception anymore. Teachers need strategies and ideas they can use right away and that make sense in diverse classrooms.

We provide professional development to thousands of educators every year and have often heard, "We've already done differentiation; now we're doing RTI (response to intervention)." Or, "It is difficult and time consuming to design tiered lessons every day." And of course, there's this response: "I think that differentiation is best used at the elementary level. By high school, students should be getting ready for college—and they sure don't differentiate there!"

Differentiation is many things to many teachers. It is a relatively simple concept with complex implementation and requires a shift in thinking and planning to be successful. It can be daunting and somewhat overwhelming when we look at all the facets, and it takes time to see the big picture.

 The Blind Men and the Elephant

The following is John Godfrey Saxe's (1816–1887) version of the famous Indian legend.

It was six men of Indostan
To learning much inclined,
Who went to see the Elephant
(Though all of them were blind),

continued →

That each by observation
Might satisfy his mind
The First approached the Elephant,
And happening to fall
Against his broad and sturdy side,
At once began to bawl:
"God bless me! but the Elephant
Is very like a wall!"
The Second, feeling of the tusk,
Cried, "Ho! what have we here
So very round and smooth and sharp?
To me 'tis mighty clear
This wonder of an Elephant
Is very like a spear!"
The Third approached the animal,
And happening to take
The squirming trunk within his hands,
Thus boldly up and spake:
"I see," quoth he, "the Elephant
Is very like a snake!"
The Fourth reached out an eager hand,
And felt about the knee.
"What most this wondrous beast is like
Is mighty plain," quoth he;
"'Tis clear enough the Elephant
Is very like a tree!"
The Fifth, who chanced to touch the ear,
Said: "E'en the blindest man
Can tell what this resembles most;
Deny the fact who can
This marvel of an Elephant
Is very like a fan!"
The Sixth no sooner had begun
About the beast to grope,
Than, seizing on the swinging tail
That fell within his scope,
"I see," quoth he, "the Elephant
Is very like a rope!"
And so these men of Indostan
Disputed loud and long,
Each in his own opinion
Exceeding stiff and strong,
Though each was partly in the right,
And all were in the wrong!
Moral:
So oft in theologic wars,
The disputants, I ween,
Rail on in utter ignorance
Of what each other mean,
And prate about an Elephant
Not one of them has seen!

Teachers often misconstrue differentiation when they have only seen one part of the differentiation elephant. A workshop on the multiple intelligences leads them to believe that they should teach to multiple intelligences. Others learn about creating tiered lessons, and that becomes their understanding of the topic, so they group most often by like readiness levels even though we know that heterogeneous groups get better results (Lou et al., 1996). Others attend a session on using data and decide they need to preassess and group students accordingly. Others believe that providing choice of assignments and assessments is the way to go.

Differentiating instruction every day for all of your students may seem like an overwhelming task. Differentiation expert Carol Ann Tomlinson's model suggests focusing on curriculum content, instructional process, and how students demonstrate their understanding through products. However, teachers often have curriculum pacing guides or programs that seem to leave little flexibility regarding instructional design, and limited time keeps teachers busy just planning lessons a week ahead. While coaching teachers over the years, we have discovered that the most helpful tools are simple, low-prep strategies that can be used daily.

In the following chapters, you will find that simple additions to how you present information to students may engage them more quickly. Orchestrating the classroom environment with brain-compatible strategies will increase the students' abilities to explore and extend the concepts and skills to be learned, and building up a repertoire of formative assessment strategies will make evaluations of student progress more accurate. We refer to these aspects as the five Es for differentiating in a brain-compatible classroom (see fig. I.1).

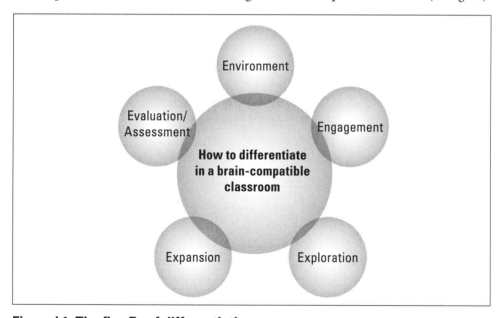

Figure I.1: The five Es of differentiation.

Differentiation may be accomplished by varying:

- How we create a safe and secure brain-compatible *environment* that maximizes student learning
- How we *engage* (hook) the learner with interesting, meaningful, relevant tasks
- How we orchestrate *exploration* of the new learning to ensure retention and mastery
- How we modify and *expand* learning to accommodate struggling learners and challenge capable students
- How we assess and *evaluate* student progress and provide feedback

This is not a simple task for a teacher given the diversity in classrooms today. Teachers are doing an amazing job, but there is always room to grow. Creating an inviting, supportive classroom environment and an instructional and assessment repertoire to provide variety and responsiveness to the learner is essential. Understanding the basics about how learning takes place is another key component for a teacher's knowledge base. Educational neuroscience is now providing teachers with some "brain basics" to help us design and orchestrate instructional strategies with the brain in mind.

Differentiation is the whole of best practice as we know it, taking the best of theory and practice and using it judiciously so all students get it. And really it's using whatever works. Differentiation is also a mindset or philosophy. It's what teachers believe about students and their commitment to all students' success. It's becoming *instructionally intelligent*. It does not have to be a complex lesson plan but a with-it-ness moment when the teacher recognizes that something different needs to be done and makes the thoughtful decision to differentiate which students need what.

What You'll Find in This Book

Differentiating instruction in any classroom with diverse learners can be a labor-intensive, daunting task—we know! Conscientious, dedicated teachers are encouraged to think big in their dreams and goals of designing differentiated instructional strategies. Our commitment in this book is to provide baby steps to reach those goals. The following chapters are filled with practical, easy-to-implement techniques that we hope teachers will find useful.

Chapter 1 provides background knowledge of brain-based teaching and learning. We summarize recent cognitive neuroscience research on how the brain learns naturally. This overview will demonstrate the need for differentiated strategies to be implemented in a safe and secure environment. Personally relevant firsthand experiences, collaboration opportunities, and active processing using a variety of intelligences and learning styles will be emphasized as key factors that address how the brain learns most effectively. The concept of teacher mindsets will be discussed as well as demystifying differentiated instruction.

In chapter 2, we explore how to create a safe and secure brain-compatible environment that maximizes student learning. We offer strategies to help you design a climate for learning and risk taking, promote an atmosphere of fun and playfulness, and encourage mindfulness and reflection. A brain- and body-compatible classroom provides alternative seating and furniture arrangements, promotes hands-on exploration, and displays clear procedures.

Chapter 3 shows you how to engage the learner with interesting, meaningful, relevant tasks. The chapter includes several strategies to stimulate the learner's interest in the topic, promote curiosity, inspire participation, and activate prior knowledge as we know that the brain seeks novelty, relevance, and meaning.

In chapter 4, we discuss how to orchestrate the exploration of new learning to ensure retention and mastery. The research relating to how brain growth and development is dependent on, and influenced by, experiences will be examined. We offer a variety of strategies to encourage investigation, provide opportunities for discovery play, enhance deep learning with multiple rehearsals, clarify concepts, define terms, chunk information, and discover patterns.

In chapter 5, we take a look at how to modify and extend learning to accommodate struggling learners and challenge capable students. Each brain is uniquely formed, and every student has developed his or her own learning preferences. Going beyond "teaching to the middle," you will discover ways to jump-start learners who are working below basic levels and load up on strategies that expand initial understanding, build depth and complexity, and extend challenges as needed for highly capable learners.

In chapter 6, we explore how to assess and evaluate student progress and provide feedback. With feedback, the brain fine-tunes neural connections and develops a sense of achievement. You will learn how to create a repertoire of preassessment and formative assessment strategies and techniques to maintain a cycle of data collection and feedback to guide instructional planning and students' next steps.

Chapter 7 provides a summary of the book's content and strategies and implementation ideas, as well as a few sample planning guides to help you get started.

We wrote this book to offer some great practical, effective, commonsense strategies that can be used immediately in the classroom and to point out some brain basics that will help you create an environment that will encourage learning. Mostly we want to provide support and encouragement as you do one of the most challenging and rewarding jobs around: teach a classroom of amazingly active, naturally curious, possibly disengaged, diverse students.

Using Educational Neuroscience to Differentiate Instruction

The argument can be made that schools are again in a time of transition—a period in which it again seems evident that one-size-fits-all approaches to curriculum and instruction are a misfit for too many students, a period in which teachers are once more trying to understand what it means to calibrate instruction based on the varying needs of an increasingly diverse student population.

—Carol Ann Tomlinson

For centuries, teachers have been challenged to address the diverse needs of all learners. As educational neuroscience becomes available to us, we can begin to understand how our students' unique brains are developing. We can use the emerging information about how learning and memory take place to inform our instructional practices on a daily basis in the classroom. Differentiation and educational neuroscience go hand in hand!

Differentiation in the General Education Classroom

Today's classrooms are filled with diverse learners with social, cultural, economic, language, and learning differences. Some students have immigrated from places far away; other students have not gone farther than a mile from their homes. Students with special needs are instructed in classrooms alongside gifted learners. Many students have been working with technology since they were toddlers; others have never used a mouse. Each student's brain has been uniquely wired. An individual's life experiences create an intricate web of memories and shape the way new learning is received.

Teachers need to welcome this diversity and seek out ways to address each student's unique needs. A traditional one-size-fits-all approach will work for a few but will likely leave many unsuccessful learners. In the past, many teachers conducted schooling in a cycle of "teach, test, and hope for the best." Many believed that if students didn't get it, it was not the teacher's fault; rather, it was due to the students' lack of effort and/or abilities. Differentiation is basically providing the opportunity for every student to succeed and reach his or her potential.

Today, we are on a quest to leave no child behind, but to achieve that end, educators must plan strategically, using all the knowledge and skills at their disposal. The process of response to intervention (RTI) has been mandated in many schools to ensure all learners have opportunities to be successful and to help educators reach students who are at risk. In the RTI model, differentiated instruction is a primary level of intervention (Bender & Shores, 2007). It is not only for those students who are struggling but also for students working at grade level and the more able, ready, and gifted students. Differentiation is necessary to meet each learner where he or she is and move him or her toward targeted standards or expectations.

Overview of RTI

In 2004, the reauthorization of the Individuals with Disabilities Education Act (IDEA) encouraged states to use the RTI process to identify and meet student learning needs. RTI is a comprehensive early detection and prevention strategy that identifies struggling students and assists them *before* they fall behind. RTI systems combine universal screening, preassessments, and high-quality instruction for all students with specific interventions targeted at struggling students. RTI involves "targeting specific areas on which students are struggling and applying increasingly intensive research-proven interventions until the threat to learning is alleviated" (Bender, 2009, p. 1). This encourages schools to provide classroom support before considering special education referrals and placements. Special education referrals are considered only for students who fail to respond to evidence-based interventions and highly effective best practices.

In RTI, the levels of interventions are referred to as "tiers." (These tiers are not to be confused with tiered lessons, a common differentiation strategy; see chapter 5.) RTI is typically thought of as having three tiers (see fig. 1.1). Tier 1 encompasses the core general education classroom instruction using high-quality, research-based best practices. Tier 2 targeted interventions are provided only to students who continue to demonstrate learning challenges and show weak progress from general education classroom instruction. Tier 2 students usually receive supplemental, small-group instruction three to five times per week aimed at building targeted skills. Tier 3 intensive interventions are provided to students who do not progress after a reasonable amount of time with Tier 2 interventions and require more personalized assistance.

In Tier 1, general education teachers differentiate instruction—including varying time, content, process, and degree of support and scaffolding—based on students' assessed skills. Helping students explore the content and skills in a variety of ways is considered

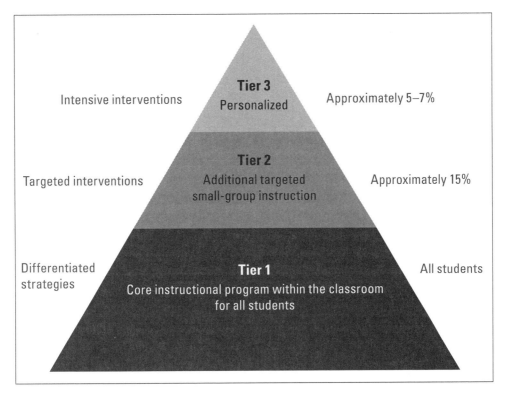

Figure 1.1: Pyramid of interventions.

the primary level of intervention and is the universal core program that all students will receive. A teacher's repertoire of differentiated strategies is key to providing opportunities for success for all students.

Quality Differentiation

As mentioned previously, the concept of differentiation can be compared to the story of the elephant and the blind men. Each man touched a different part of the elephant and described the elephant based on what he touched—as a rope, fan, snake, wall, spear, or tree—each with an accurate definition based on his understanding and exposure to the elephant. There are many facets to differentiated instruction, and if you just touch one part, you are missing others. Some glom on to the idea of choice boards or tic-tac-toe charts, and others emphasize flexible grouping. Those who zero in on one of these differentiated strategies may be missing the big picture; the whole is sometimes not quite clear or consolidated. And then, of course, there are others who think, "Differentiation? Oh yes, we've done that already!"

Differentiation is not just a set of strategies, although you certainly need an instructional repertoire in order to differentiate. Differentiation encompasses many things but basically evolves from a core philosophy or mindset that all students have potential and can be successful. Carol Ann Tomlinson (2010), a recognized author and expert in educational differentiation, believes that there are at least five indicators of quality differentiation:

1. A positive or growth mindset about student potential
2. Teacher-student connections to support learning
3. Developing community
4. High-quality curriculum as the target for virtually all students
5. Assessment to inform instruction (pp. 252–256)

Since the late 1990s, Tomlinson's model has been the foundation for the understanding of various elements of differentiated instruction:

> There are at least three classroom elements that teachers can modify in response to student readiness, interest, and learning profile needs. Those are (1) content, (2) process, and (3) product. . . . Purposeful modifications of these elements, informed by ongoing assessment information, enhance the likelihood of each student's academic success. (Tomlinson, 2010, p. 258)

Many teachers, although cognizant of the research and acknowledging the need to differentiate, are often overwhelmed by the task of differentiating and thus don't know what to do or where to begin. Collecting and analyzing assessment data, meeting with professional learning communities, modifying lessons for struggling learners, adapting tasks for students with disabilities, and preparing for engaging lessons add up to more than a full-time job. However, the awareness of the need for differentiation and the desire to help each student reach his or her potential are wonderful places to begin. In this book, we provide many easy-to-use strategies to help teachers think big but start small.

Brain-Compatible Classrooms

Understanding how the brain operates can influence how educators teach. In the 1980s, research and new theories about how the brain works emerged. Although initially much of the research involved nonhuman studies, the new information influenced our understanding of how human brains grow, develop, and learn. Then, with modern imaging techniques, a door was opened to the internal workings of the human brain. As this research emerged, many thoughtful educators began to use the information to create classrooms and learning experiences that were believed to be more brain-friendly.

The field of educational neuroscience continues to grow as researchers gather data and understand various aspects of how human brains learn, use language, calculate, approach tasks, and process new concepts into long-term memory. Many of the studies are very specific and have begun to help us understand the neural underpinnings of autism, dyslexia, attention disorders, and so on. While many neuroscientists are hesitant to suggest that recent brain research has direct application to education, we believe it is possible to draw implications and make some generalizations, and we dare to suggest some commonsense implementation strategies for brain-compatible classroom practice. A handful of educational leaders have investigated the emerging theories and acted as brain research "interpreters." Geoffrey and Renate Caine, Robert Sylwester, Pat Wolfe, David Sousa, Barbara

Given, and Eric Jensen have been our mentors and helped create a bridge from the research laboratories to the classrooms.

According to John G. Geake (2009), a professor and cofounder of the Oxford Cognitive Neuroscience Education Forum:

> Neuroscientific findings, appropriately filtered and interpreted, can be, and possibly should be, of professional interest to educators, especially school teachers and teacher-educators. . . . Relevant and useful professional and classroom applications of educational neuroscience will increasingly become available as we gradually come to understand more about brain function through neuroscience research which answers educational questions about learning, memory, motivation, and so on. (p. 10)

Some call the emerging model "brain-based learning," others "brain-compatible teaching." Whatever it is termed, it is simply incorporating brain-friendly strategies in the classroom. Ultimately the composite model provides educators with some guidelines about teaching strategies and learning environments that could maximize how their students' brains learn.

The brain's purpose is not to go to school, but to survive day to day, minute by minute. The brain's basic innate tasks from birth are to get upright, become mobile, meet basic needs, and communicate (Gregory, 2005). Humans also strive to develop trust in interpersonal relationships (Goleman, 2006b). Classrooms and schools need to be places where the brain is supported in its quest. If a student is focused on his or her basic needs or is physically uncomfortable, he or she is not able to attend to the learning that should be taking place. When students are asked to remain seated and silent and to compete against their peers, they may become overly stressed, and when there is unmanageable stress, thinking and learning are minimized. The learner is no longer functioning in the cerebral cortex (thinking and rational brain area); instead, he or she is in survival mode, resulting in limited language or thought processing and a basic fight, flight, or freeze reflex response (Gregory, 2005; Zull, 2002; Posner & Rothbart, 2007).

People do their best "when they experience both high motivation and manageable stress; when people are undermotivated or overstressed, their performance suffers" (Goleman, 2006b, p. 77). This relationship between stress (arousal) and performance is known as the Yerkes-Dodson law of arousal and can be illustrated with a simple inverted U shape (see fig. 1.2, page 14).

With little stress, or arousal, there will be a low level of performance. As the stress increases, in most cases, one will experience a greater level of performance. And then, it peaks. Neuroscientist Antonio Damasio (2003) refers to this plateau as "maximal cognitive efficiency." No matter how much more arousal or stress the individual experiences, his or her performance and capabilities will not improve. They may, in fact, begin to decline as the pressure continues to be exerted. Relentless stress, discomfort, or incongruity will cause the performance to reach a threshold and then begin to falter. At this point, the learner may become defensive, unresponsive, or apathetic, and success diminishes rapidly.

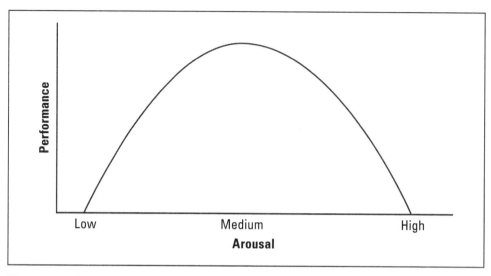

Figure 1.2: The Yerkes-Dodson law of arousal.

When all students are asked to perform the same task, each will react individually with a range from excitement to boredom or frustration. What excites or engages one student may be too demanding for another and may cause undue stress and anxiety. Offering choices and options may lower stress levels for students and give them a sense of control, which can be very motivating.

Mihaly Csikszentmihalyi (1990), a Hungarian cognitive psychologist, refers to the state of optimal engagement as "flow," in which the following conditions exist:

- Appropriate challenge is offered just beyond one's existing skill level.
- People can exercise a sense of control in the process or product to be created.
- Feedback is available as needed.
- People feel relaxed as well as alert and engaged. Stress is reduced.
- People persist because success is incremental and encouraging.
- The participant is tenacious and motivated.

Csikszentmihalyi's flow zone is illustrated as a perfect balance between challenge and skill. If the task is too difficult for the learner's perceived abilities, anxiety will emerge. If the task is not challenging enough, the learner may become bored. As the task or activity continues, there should be a gradual increase in skill development as the task becomes more difficult.

Keeping each student within his or her flow zone and working at peak performance is a mammoth challenge for a teacher with a classroom full of diverse learners, but by paying attention to student learning profiles, preferences, and interests, and by using differentiated strategies that give students options, the teacher has a better chance of orchestrating flow.

We have been implementing brain-compatible techniques in our respective classrooms and conducting action research for over two decades and have determined some basic principles that will help educators provide an engaging environment and opportunities for the brain to make meaning.

Seven Common Brain Principles for Educators

Two common brain facts often shared by neuroscientists are:

1.   The optimal number of bits of information that the brain can manage in working memory at any given time appears to be seven (with a +/− 2 variable).

2.   The brain may be able to store more items if we combine, or chunk, several separate bits of information into bite-sized manageable pieces or categories.

There is a vast amount of neuroscience research that might be of interest to educators. To make this information more manageable, we have chunked it into seven common principles that can guide teachers as they design brain-friendly learning environments.

Principle 1: Brains Operate in Response to Patterns or Schemata

The brain makes sense of new information using probability based on previous experiences and develops schemata, which are patterns that are stored together and understood. Chaining is the process of making connections by finding similarities (Ratey, 2008). Well-known pediatrician and author Mel Levine (1990) calls this "horizontal threading." The brain searches its filing system to find other concepts and ideas that may be connected to the new information, trying to make sense of it. The brain has no time for useless patterns and pieces of information that do not mesh with what it already knows or finds interesting. By identifying like attributes of ideas, the brain develops concepts. Pattern seeking is common to every brain, but prior experiences are unique and specific to each person.

Meaning comes from making connections between the unknown and the familiar, and without schemata (background knowledge), students' connections are not complete. Teachers can encourage pattern making by:

♦   Preassessing students regarding their prior knowledge (by helping students access previously learned information, they may be able to detect patterns they have already experienced and connect these to the new information or skills)

♦   Routinely pointing out patterns and repetitions within content and skills

♦   Making real-world connections to new learning and concepts

♦   Organizing classroom routines and rituals to establish daily patterns of behavior

♦   Providing students with advance organizers and note-taking templates with headings or concepts organized (chunked) by attributes

Principle 2: How One Feels Makes the Difference in Learning

Emotions make the brain pay attention and can either enhance or inhibit the ability to learn. When experiencing a dangerous or stressful situation, the brain's default system for emergencies kicks into high gear. Negative emotions and stress can minimize learning. Positive emotional experiences can create memories of a successful outcome and generate a feeling of competence and interest (Ornstein & Sobel, 1987; Pert, 1997; Damasio, 1994).

Emotions may also play a key role in tagging new memories. The neurotransmitters, such as dopamine, that are released during positive emotionally charged events actually facilitate long-term memory formation (Pert, 1997). These emotional hooks appear to have a vital role in helping children later make decisions and apply what they have learned in school to real-life situations (Pert, 1997). Mary Helen Immordino-Yang and Antonio Damasio (2007) suggest, "When we educators fail to appreciate the importance of students' emotions, we fail to appreciate a critical force in students' learning" (p. 9).

Powerful learning occurs through rich emotional experiences that engage thinking as well as feelings. Great teachers know that, in addition to having basic needs met, emotions and feelings affect a student's performance and learning. As previously noted, student success depends on feeling safe, secure, and comfortable in a positive and congenial environment. Laughter, joy, and playfulness within a classroom will enhance students' moods, states of mind, and learning capacity.

Principle 3: All the Senses Enrich Learning

Richard Mayer (2010), a psychology professor at the University of California, Santa Barbara, has conducted many experiments to show that learners in multisensory environments do better than students who receive input via only one of the senses. When multiple senses are used during the learning process, memory is more accurate and the information is retained for a longer period of time (Medina, 2008).

In order to grow dendrites, the delicate branches connecting neurons, brains need enriched environments that stimulate all of the senses. Multiple repetitions strengthen the dendrites and synaptic connections between neurons. This stimulation increases the speed of recalling information or performing a task. The ability to recall information can be enhanced by elaborating the initial encoding. Involving a variety of the senses and processing new concepts through visual, auditory, and kinesthetic pathways greatly increase the chance of the learner filing the new learning in ways that make later retrieval easier (Medina, 2008). This premise also supports the five natural learning systems described by Barbara Given (2002)—social, emotional, cognitive, physical, and reflective—and tends to be true for all learners.

Connecting the whole body to the learning experience will help students who have strengths in auditory, visual, and tactile/kinesthetic areas. The more we can actively engage body and mind, the more learning will take place. So hands-on, physically engaging learning experiences such as role playing and model construction will engage more learners and facilitate meaning and concept development (Hanniford, 2005).

Clinical psychiatrist John Ratey (2008) has shown that any exercise can activate neural connections, lower stress, focus thinking, and actually enhance the memory process. Exercise increases blood volume in an area of the brain near the hippocampus, a region associated with memory formation. Research also is showing that physical activity stimulates the production of brain-derived neurotrophic factor (BDNF), a powerful growth factor for our cells. Ratey has discovered that BDNF acts like Miracle-Gro on certain neurons in the brain—especially those near the hippocampus. The more you exercise, the more usable BDNF you create, keeping existing cells healthy and promoting neurogenesis—the formation of new cells in the brain.

Principle 4: We Learn Best When It's Meaningful and Interesting

Humans instinctively seek to understand and make sense of their world. This innate quest is both conscious and unconscious. It is a natural human phenomenon to be continuously learning, seeking, and being curious about the world around us (Smilkstein, 2003). We respond to novelty, meaning, and relevance. What we experience promotes dendritic growth and brain development (Diamond & Hopson, 1998).

Teachers should try to create a learning environment that provides some familiarity as well as flexibility, challenge, and exploratory opportunities. Interesting and relevant topics and activities are critical to capture the attention of the learner. Educators can provide opportunities for students to channel their search for meaning, relevance, and understanding and help them focus by using contracts, projects, questions, and inquiries that have real-world applications.

Principle 5: We Learn Better Together in a Safe Environment

Humans need to connect, collaborate, and cooperate (Panksepp, 1998). Everyone comes complete with what Alison Gopnik, Andrew Meltzoff, and Patricia Kuhl (1999) call the "contact urge." People seek the company of others at times and prefer being independent in other situations (Covey, 1989). Everyone seeks a sense of belonging and a community where they are included and respected.

Social interaction is critical for normal neurocognitive development. Adolescence may be a key time to develop the social skills and social networks in the brain as the brain is undergoing a reorganization and new skills can be fostered and developed (Blakemore, Burnett, & Dahl, 2010). No matter how engaging a DVD or computer program may be, face-to-face interaction is key for the development of language, social skills, and empathy. Time with technology shouldn't take away from possible real interactions. Social intelligence is described as being emotionally self-aware (being able to identify one's emotional state, regulate stress, experience joyfulness, and manage upsets) as well as understanding social skills. One who is socially intelligent is able to read other people's faces and gestures to understand their emotions and mental states. No matter how convenient teleconferencing may seem, face-to-face social interaction is still the most powerful means of communication.

Recent neuroscience research of mirror neurons suggests that we each have the ability to feel another's emotional state and empathize with him or her by automatically adjusting our own feelings: "Emotional states are contagious, brain-to-brain . . . Mirror neurons create, within a person's brain, a replica of the brain state of whomever that person is with" (Goleman, 2006b, p. 78).

Because we now know that emotions can be contagious, "role modeling matters more than ever. Mirror neurons really support the importance of role modeling because we know that people can learn by seeing someone execute well. We now understand the mechanism: when you watch someone else perform, that elicits the same arousal pattern in you" (Freedman, 2007).

Oral communication in the classroom is essential. This can be especially a concern for those interpersonal learners who need to dialogue and share ideas and talk out their thinking with others. Of course, procedures need to be in place to provide some guidelines for sharing ideas. There also needs to be a supportive tone in the classroom, a sense of inclusiveness, to alleviate undue stress or perceived threats.

Principle 6: Everything Affects Learning

We are all concerned with making meaning of our world (Sylwester, 1995). Everything from the environment's decor and orderliness to an individual's body language and facial cues is registered consciously or unconsciously in the brain. The brain is continually scanning and evaluating its surroundings.

Based on extensive research by Michael Posner and Mary Rothbart (2007), we understand the brain to be a sequential processor of incoming information. There are three basic networks active in our brain all of the time. They respond sequentially to input perceived in our sensory environment. Our arousal system alerts us to any unusual events or new activities. This triggers our orienting network to pay attention and examine the situation for more data. Finally our executive network, involving our cerebral cortex, helps us determine our next plan of action and voluntary response. This sequence of detect, orient, and decide is a pattern that repeats itself nonstop during our waking hours.

There are two main types of attention. Stimulus-driven attention is when the brain notices input that may indicate a survival issue, such as movement, sound, color, light, pain, or such. All attention is then directed to the stimuli until the brain is assured that the potential threat or danger has passed. Goal-driven attention is when the brain takes on a task or activity that is relevant, meaningful, and interesting to the learner. With high interest, the student may be capable of ignoring internal and external distractions and inhibit other sensory stimulation. All energy would be directed to the task at hand (Medina, 2008).

Some believe that the ability to actually multitask is a myth: "We are biologically incapable of processing attention-rich inputs simultaneously" (Medina, 2008, p. 85). Bouncing back and forth between two tasks may be exhausting, and productivity goes down for each task. This creates a state of continuous partial attention. For students, this is often an unproductive time. Students may need help organizing their time, materials, and tasks to make decisions and complete steps.

Students also need quiet time to digest and reflect on their learning. Learning metacognitive skills can help students build their self-awareness and their abilities to exert effortful control. Help students orchestrate quiet time during the day, or create a place in the room that might serve as an interruption-free zone. Turning off technology and removing other distractions will help most kids (and adults!) get more done.

Everything we say or do either pulls students toward us or pushes them away. Our tone of voice, the colorful displays and support structures we install in our classrooms, our enthusiasm and concern—all these things influence students at the unconscious level. The brain is susceptible to conscious and unconscious information, and often nonverbal communication is more powerful than verbal.

Principle 7: Each Brain Is Wired Differently

Every brain is unique, even though they operate in similar ways. The uniqueness is a result of both heredity and the environment in which we have been raised. Genetics do play a role in brain growth and development, but many neuroscientists have determined that environmental factors may have an even greater influence (Shaw et al., 2006). As a result of these differences, we have different likes and dislikes in many areas, including how we prefer to learn.

Elliot Eisner (1983), professor emeritus of art and education at Stanford University School of Education, postulates that the difference between the art of teaching and just the craft is the teacher's willingness and ability to continue to garner additional teaching strategies and techniques to reach all learners. This makes the teacher more of a facilitator than a giver of information.

Today's students want to learn differently than those of the past. Marc Prensky (2010), author of *Teaching Digital Natives*, states that students "want to create, using the tools of their time" (p. 2). As educators, we have a responsibility to try to understand how our students' brains are wired. What will the art of teaching look like in the information age?

21st Century Brains

Our students were born into the age of technology and are part of the Net Generation. "Digital" is their first language, and thus, they are known as "digital natives." They were born with a mouse in their hands, and it has been estimated that they immerse themselves in interactive digital technology possibly fifty hours per week. The Kaiser Family Foundation (2010) reported the following:

> Over the past five years, young people have increased the amount of time they spend consuming media by an hour and seventeen minutes daily, from 6:21 to 7:38—almost the amount of time most adults spend at work each day, except that young people use media seven days a week instead of five. Moreover, given the amount of time they spend using more than one medium at a time, today's youth pack a total of 10 hours and 45 minutes worth of media content into those daily 7½ hours—an increase of almost 2¼ hours of media exposure per day over the past five years (since 2004). (p. 2)

Frequent and continual usage of a particular brain region can lead to that area's development, increasing its size, density, and efficiency. Don Tapscott (2009), in his book *Grown Up Digital*, reports that researchers studied video game players' brains to see if their visual processing area was more developed. Experienced game players noticed more and could process rapid-fire visual information better than non-game players. They went on to show that by playing video games daily for twelve consecutive days, even non-game players could improve their visual processing abilities. Our students' brains are wired differently from ours, and our instructional strategies and classroom organization need to recognize these new and "improved" brains.

Despite much controversy, not all of the technology exposure is detrimental to young people's brains. These digital natives have defined a new culture of communication and are globally networked. Their brains are wired for rapid-fire cyber searches. They've learned to quickly focus their attention, skim for information, analyze the data, and then instantaneously make a decision to go on or not (Prensky, 2010).

However, an inordinate amount of screen time could keep children away from opportunities to play outside, exercise, and have face-to-face interactions with others, and the ability to read for deep comprehension and complexity may not be well developed as students become expert skimmers of information (Small & Vorgan, 2008). Using technology often puts our brains in a state of continuous partial attention, making it difficult to stay fully engaged and stick with something. After long periods of working on computers, many people experience techno-brain burnout. They report feeling irritable, fatigued, and easily distracted.

So what should educators do? Richard Louv (2011), in his book *The Nature Principle*, suggests that we have to develop in students what he refers to as a "hybrid mind": "The best preparation for the twenty-first century may be a combination of natural and virtual experience" (p. 38). As teachers, we will have to keep navigating a delicate balance of digital integration into our classroom practices, while encouraging and providing real-world experiences, face-to-face interactions, and personal skills regarding how to maintain healthy minds and bodies.

Children's brains think and learn differently. As we take on the task of teaching 21st century learners, we must research how our students' brains are wired and then begin to work on how our brains can facilitate powerful learning.

Finding the Learner's Sweet Spot

Recognizing that all students differ is paramount to helping all students be successful. Neuroscientists Sarah-Jayne Blakemore and Uta Frith (2005) believe that in the future, more research will also help us understand what is going on inside the teacher's brain in the classroom and that "at a minimum, teaching may just mean providing people with the right opportunities and encouraging them to take up these opportunities" (p. 149).

When involved in an inspired moment of learning, students experience an intersection of focused attention, high interest, a connection to prior successes, and positive feelings. We call this the learner's sweet spot (see fig. 1.3)—an elusive holy grail that, when discovered and nudged by an empowered teacher, can change everything for a student. Teachers can find each student's sweet spot for learning by surveying prior knowledge, determining how success was achieved in the past, and ultimately predicting what degree of interest the student has in the task.

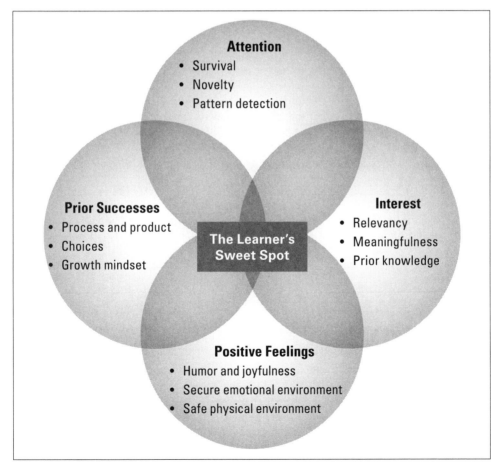

Figure 1.3: The learner's sweet spot.

To determine the elements of a learner's sweet spot, the teacher must gather information about the learner by using a formal student profile, collecting informal anecdotal observations, or simply executing a trial-and-error approach. We believe teachers can determine and target each learner's sweet spot by investigating four areas of prior experiences. The areas to consider are:

1. **Positive feelings**. Does the learner have positive feelings and memories about the type of task or activity to be done? Does the learner have a history of prior successes with learning and school?

   a. Determine whether the emotional climate and tone of the classroom are conducive to this learner's needs and anxiety threshold.

   b. Orchestrate the physical environment and integrate opportunities to move around to provide a level of comfort for the learner.

   c. Create and maintain an aura of joyfulness, playfulness, and positive regard for all within the classroom.

2. **Attention**. What types of stimuli are most likely to attract and engage this particular learner?

   a. Assess and consider the age range and maturity level of the student.

   b. Ensure that the student's basic needs have been met and opportunities to eat, drink, move, and stretch have been worked into the activity.

   c. Seek out opportunities for the student to interact with technology as part of the lesson based on the learner's experience with technology.

3. **Interest**. Does the learner have adequate prior knowledge? Will he or she find the concept or content to be relevant? Is it personally meaningful?

   a. Create a hook to something the student is interested in exploring.

   b. Preassess to determine the student's prior experience and interest with the topic.

   c. Create a reason to investigate this subject—something that may be meaningful in the future.

4. **Prior successes**. Has the learner had prior positive experiences with the type of task or activity to be completed? Has the learner demonstrated a preference for particular choice activities or processing opportunities (visual, auditory, kinesthetic, or multiple intelligences)?

   a. Preassess to determine the degree of familiarity and foundational knowledge the student has about the topic.

   b. Refer to the student's profile to determine if he or she has demonstrated success processing in a particular way in prior activities.

 c. Consider how choices might be given using a variety of process and product possibilities to attract each student.

People learn best when they are comfortable, feeling safe and confident in their own skin. It is easier for students to learn in their preferred styles or modes, utilizing their strengths. Teaching to the students' sweet spots considers the cognitive, affective, physiological, and psychological needs of the students, how they perceive and process information, and how they engage with, interact with, and react to their surroundings and environment.

Catering to students' interests also promotes positive connections between student and teacher (Willingham, 2009). By understanding students' sweet spots and learning preferences, educators can differentiate instruction to appeal to, engage, and facilitate learning for students with different prior experiences and readiness levels.

So What About Learning Styles?

Many theories and models for describing learning differences and styles have been proposed. Sousa and Tomlinson (2011) note, "Neuroscientific research has discovered limited evidence to support the idea that individuals actually learn in different ways by using different neural networks to accomplish similar learning tasks" (p. 147). While there may not be conclusive brain research to help us understand why students have preferences and develop specific learning styles, teachers know that every student has learning preferences. By understanding a student's range of prior experiences, successes, and failures, a teacher may be able to better serve him or her with diverse intellectual ways of receiving, processing, and applying new information and skills. Teachers can expand their instructional tackle box by putting themselves in their students' shoes.

There are several models educators can use to help recognize a student's learning preferences. One such model was introduced by professors Kenneth Dunn and Rita Dunn (1987). They suggested a learning-styles model that categorized personal styles into auditory, visual, tactile, and kinesthetic.

Auditory Learners

Speaking and listening appeal to auditory learners. Engagement and absorption happen through discussion and interaction. Auditory learners want to share their learning with other students. They like to listen and appreciate the sound of their own voices as well.

Visual Learners

Illustrations, diagrams, charts, and pictures appeal to visual learners. Visual learners like to use graphic organizers so that they can incorporate symbolism and color to create long-term meaning and understanding. Visual stimuli connect in their memory and create visions in the mind's eye. Visual learners recall ideas and concepts that have been presented in a visual way or for which they have created symbolic or pictorial representations.

Tactile Learners

Touching and handling concrete materials and manipulatives appeal to tactile learners. They like to write, draw, and get their hands on the learning. When they ask to see something, they want to touch it. These are often the students who tap pencils and doodle, as their hands need to be busy to engage their minds. They are mildly kinesthetic learners, and creating models and constructing samples allow their muscles to make memories.

Kinesthetic Learners

Being able to physically get involved in the learning through movement and application is appealing to kinesthetic learners. They appreciate being involved in drama, simulations, and role playing. Opportunities to use their whole bodies to learn and participate are important to them. "Sitting and getting" bores and frustrates these learners, and they will become disengaged when their needs aren't met. Such frustration and stress can cause the release of adrenaline and cortisol in the bloodstream, which can be harmful to the cardiovascular system over time. Physical movement helps reduce the level of cortisol in the bloodstream (Ratey, 2008).

Appealing to All Learners

In differentiated classrooms, all learners should have adequate time to engage in their preferred mode of learning. It's not recommended that educators label students, though they should consider the different styles of learning as they design and implement instruction. Many students' learning preferences are dynamic and change in relationship to the task at hand or evolve with maturity. Providing a variety of ways to interact and elaborative rehearsal using different methods to evoke the senses will increase the chances that all learners have an opportunity to make sense and meaning of the content and that information and skills will move into long-term memory. To thoughtful teachers, learning preferences and styles are "not a method of restrictive teaching, but a reminder of the benefits of explicit mixed modality pedagogy" (Geake, 2009, p. 75).

Gardner's Multiple Intelligences Theory

Since 1984, many educators have found Howard Gardner's multiple intelligences theory to be a helpful model to chunk various processing and problem-solving strategies. Although not well grounded in neuroscience (musical-rhythmic intelligence doesn't show up in the brain on an MRI!), the eight intelligences provide a conceptual framework, vocabulary, and corresponding product suggestions that remind and help teachers to differentiate instructional processes and products. Gardner suggests that rather than a fixed IQ, people have a range of different propensities of intelligence that allows them to solve problems, handle crises, and create things of value for their culture. Following are brief descriptions of the eight intelligences.

The first two are communication intelligences.

1. **Verbal-linguistic**. Communication is important to people with high levels of verbal intelligence. They value opportunities to become involved in debates, storytelling, and reciting poetry. They enjoy reading and appreciate metaphors, puns, analogies, and similes, and become immersed in the language. They are often auditory learners and choose to listen, speak, read, and write. They enjoy many methods of communication—letters, faxes, emails, tweeting, and blogging on computers and cell phones. New technological ways of communicating just enhance their communication skills. Verbal and language skills are essential in our world. Media personnel, journalists, editors, actors, writers, and orators excel in this area.

2. **Musical-rhythmic**. People with a high level of this intelligence appreciate the rhyme, rhythm, melody, and beat of poetry and music. They appreciate and respond to a variety of rhythm sources. You often see these students tapping out a beat. They learn and work best when able to listen to music or use rhythm or rhyme to help in the memory process. People with a high degree of musical-rhythmic intelligence often have careers in theater, as musicians, as poets, or as lyricists.

The next four are object-related intelligences.

3. **Logical-mathematical**. Developing patterns, using numbers, recognizing cause and effect, and organizing and sequencing ideas and things intrigue logical-mathematical learners. They use logic, reasoning, and data to solve problems, pose hypotheses, and create rationales. Mathematicians, programmers, investigators, and lawyers are highly developed in the area of logical-mathematical intelligence.

4. **Visual-spatial**. People with this intelligence are able to see detail, appreciate color and symbols, and often use charts and representations to interpret and demonstrate their understanding of new information or concepts. These learners are successful with using visualization to enhance the memory process. They usually have an innate aptitude for navigation based on spatial relationships and visual clues. Engineers and architects, artists and sculptors, videographers, filmmakers, and directors rely on their visual-spatial intelligence in their crafts.

5. **Bodily-kinesthetic**. A heightened sense and awareness of one's own body and highly developed fine and/or gross muscle dexterity are evident in people with this intelligence. They appreciate manipulating materials, are eager to apply

ideas and concepts in a concrete way rather than using paper and pencil, and value action-oriented activities. Bodily-kinesthetic learners excel in vocations such as sports, acting, and medicine.

6. **Naturalist**. Naturalists appreciate and honor the world and nature, including all species of flora and fauna. Nature's patterns and details are noticed, classified, and organized by the discerning naturalist. These practices carry over into other aspects of their lives. Environmentalist and botanist are careers that might attract naturalists.

The last two intelligences relate to the self and social preferences.

7. **Interpersonal**. People with a high degree of this intelligence have highly evolved social skills. They are generally sensitive and empathetic to others, able to interpret the moods and feelings of those around them. They are valuable members of a team. Coaching, mediation, and counseling are natural fits for this intelligence.

8. **Intrapersonal**. Intrapersonal learners are usually quite introspective. They have the ability to recognize and manage their own emotions and feelings and use this knowledge to adjust their moods and behaviors. They use metacognition to self-assess and set goals. They are able to identify their strengths, admit their needs, and self-direct and correct.

Gardner has also suggested the possibility of a ninth intelligence referred to as "existential." Existential learners are those who are sensitive to the introspection of their reason for being. They reflect on questions such as "Why am I here?" "What contribution do I make?" "What is the meaning of life?" and "What will be my legacy?" They use deep thinking, self-reflection, and meditation to examine these themes. Gardner hasn't as yet identified this as a true intelligence as it doesn't fulfill all the identification criteria.

Through our own action research, we have had great success using the multiple intelligences theory as a way to provide choice activities and learning tasks that appeal to our students. This way, all students are working in their areas of strength at times, and sometimes, they are stretching in areas they have yet to develop. This success also gives them a sense of efficacy and confidence so that they feel better about tackling more difficult learning tasks. The endorphins—natural feel-good chemicals—in their brains are increased, and their memories are enhanced. When we determine a student's sweet spot, we might find the language of multiple intelligences helpful in planning differentiated instructional strategies.

Teacher Mindsets

What are your goals as an educator this year? Do you have high hopes for *all* of your students? Is this one of those years that you hope to just make it through? Are you frustrated by students' lack of engagement and prior knowledge? How do you maintain your motivation to teach? Perhaps you are a cheerleader for your professional learning community, continually urging others to try new strategies, stay motivated despite funding cutbacks, and maintain a hopeful attitude with recalcitrant students. Maybe you are over-whelmed by the demands of the disinterested students, new administration, and difficult (or absent) parents. It's worth taking a moment to reflect on your personal motivation and views about student learning.

Carol Dweck, a researcher and Stanford psychology professor, is an expert on motiva-tion and intelligence. In her book *Mindset: The New Psychology of Success* (2006), she dis-cusses how many people view intelligence and where ability comes from. According to Dweck, people fall along a continuum between "fixed" and "growth" according to their view of intelligence and success. Those who believe their success and abilities are a result of hard work and learning are described as having a growth mindset. These people are more likely to keep working hard despite setbacks. They don't mind failure so much because they know that they can improve their performance if given another chance. Those who believe that they are born with an innate ability that has limits are described as having a fixed mindset. These people are more likely to dread failure because it confirms and exposes their limited capabilities in certain areas. They give up easily when challenged because they believe that no matter how hard they try, it is futile to try to change their personal limitations. Effective teachers have positive mindsets that guide their behavior through-out the teaching and learning processes (Brooks & Goldstein, 2008).

Dweck believes that educational experiences and classroom interactions may contrib-ute to a child's mindset development. Subtle comments regarding students' performance may influence how they begin to view themselves as successful (or unsuccessful) learn-ers. When a teacher gives a praise statement, such as "Good job! You are really smart!" the learner's fixed mindset is more likely to be reinforced. Teachers who use compliments and encouragement such as "Good job! You are working hard!" may help students develop a growth mindset. The student's mindset about his or her own capabilities can be enhanced or hindered by the teacher's mindset about the student's abilities (see table 1.1, page 28.)

Environment is a contributor to the development of mindsets as "more than 30 years of study show that children raised in growth-mindset homes consistently outscored their fixed-mindset peers in academic achievement. They do better in adult life too. That's not surprising" (Medina, 2010, p. 140). Teachers and parents can help children develop a growth mindset, also known as a fluid mindset, by encouraging them to persist and to think about learning as a lifelong pursuit.

Take a moment to reflect on your mindset about learning. Do you believe that by the time students reach you their abilities are already determined by genetics, experiences, and environment? Are you teaching with the assumption that not all students will be able to learn? A fixed mindset regarding learning and intelligence may limit your abilities to effectively apply differentiated instructional strategies. Staying motivated to seek out and implement a variety of learning opportunities for all students is dependent on a growth mindset about intelligence. Do you believe that every student can continue learning this year? Do you believe that each child can grow, with hard work, multiple chances, perse-verance, and a variety of strategies?

Table 1.1: Fixed and Growth Mindsets of Teachers and Students

Mindset	Teachers	Students
Fixed	• Believe that "smart" or "not smart" is innate • Believe that genes and environment ultimately determine one's potential • Frequently separate students based on abilities • Believe students have permanent traits and frequently make evaluations	• See themselves as "smart" or "not smart" • Believe that their parents' abilities (or lack of) and backgrounds have determined their potential • Believe that if they don't learn something quickly, they are not smart • Believe that if they are smart, they don't need to put out much effort
Growth	• Interested in helping students develop their many abilities • Provide multiple opportunities for learning • Believe students can overcome all obstacles and be successful	• Believe they can learn from mistakes • Are motivated to try again and work harder • Know that their parents and circumstances do not determine who they are or what they can become

Educational systems and classrooms that continue to track or level student groupings may actually be reinforcing a fixed mindset for students. By the time they reach the middle grades, students may be apathetic and frustrated: "Why even try? I'm always going to be a buzzard." Or, "I don't have to work hard; school is easy for me." Classrooms that celebrate learning differences, promote learning in a variety of ways, and acknowledge that each learner may be on a different timetable for mastery reinforce the growth mindset.

Think Big, Start Small

Your success in implementing differentiated strategies will be aligned with your current mindset—and your willingness to consider a possible shift in thinking. Teachers who have fluid, growth mindsets regarding learning continually think big about their students' potential: they recognize the vast possibilities for instruction; they are willing to seek out differentiated strategies that may help students continue to grow and learn; they design their classrooms to accommodate students' needs and identify their learning sweet spots; and relationships and conversations are encouraging and supportive when successes are experienced as well as when challenges are encountered. Think big when you visualize how you will orchestrate possibilities for students to learn.

Although you may be motivated to provide multiple opportunities for students to learn, start small! Teachers with growth mindsets may try to satisfy all students' unique needs and ultimately frustrate themselves and their students. Shifting to a mindset of a more student-centered classroom in which differentiation is part of the thinking and planning may be an easy transition for some teachers. Others may have greater success by selecting just a few of the suggestions found in the following chapters and starting slowly. Just get started, and you will find you are doing more each week, each month, and each year.

Do it all, just not all at once!

Chapter Review

Differentiated Instruction in General Education: A discussion of why differentiated instruction is part of the general education classroom.

- Social, cultural, and economic diversity, *page 9*
- Overview of RTI, *page 10*

Quality Differentiated Instruction: What is quality differentiation? This concept is defined with indicators and elements explained.

- "The Blind Men and the Elephant," *page 11*
- Clarity regarding definition of differentiation, *page 11*
- Five indicators and three elements, *page 12*

Brain-Compatible Classrooms: Clarifies what we mean by a brain-compatible classroom, particularly regarding the following:

- Neuroscience and education, *page 12*
- Law of arousal, *page 13*
- Flow, *page 14*
- Seven common brain principles, *page 15*

21st Century Brains: Explores what we know about the brains that are coming to class these days.

- Digital natives, *page 19*
- Sweet spot, *page 21*

Learning Styles: Discusses how learners differ from one another in ways and preferences for learning.

- Auditory, visual, tactile, kinesthetic, *page 23*
- Multiple intelligences, *page 24*

Teacher Mindsets: Mindsets have a definite impact on the success of differentiation in the classroom.

◆   Fixed or growth, *page 26*

Think Big, Start Small: Suggests a way of beginning or continuing the implementation of differentiation in classrooms and schools, *page 28*

Creating a Brain-Compatible Environment

One thing that brain research tells us—loud and clear—is that the way we raise and teach our children not only helps shape their brains, but can also influence or even alter the way genes play out their roles. This promising news also means, however, that we have a serious obligation to attend to factors over which we have some control— namely, most things that happen to children at home and at school throughout their growing-up years.

—Jane M. Healy

To effectively implement differentiation strategies, teachers must design and orchestrate a brain-compatible environment. We believe that educators can interpret and apply some basic tenets from neuroscience research to create classrooms that are in line with how natural learning occurs. In this chapter, we offer a variety of simple suggestions that can help transform any classroom into a place where students feel safe, secure, challenged, motivated, successful, included, and independent. As previously discussed, it will be important to determine each student's sweet spot related to a learning environment that is perfect for him or her. For instance, some learners have seating preferences; other students have lighting or sound preferences. Our challenge as educators is to provide the general ambiance with options/nuances to better satisfy each learner's needs.

The basic categories to consider when designing a brain-compatible classroom are:

◆ Physical environment—lights, noise, air

◆ Basic needs—hunger, thirst, fatigue, exercise

◆ Systems and patterns—agendas, procedures, self-help strategies for independence

- Stress management—managing emotions, breaks, coping skills
- Social connections—inclusion, tribes, partners

Physical Environment

Many students may be sensitive to physical aspects of the classroom. Lack of natural light, ambient noise from air systems and technology, and air temperature and quality may all cause learners' brains to be distracted from learning and engagement. Classrooms that lack a comfortable climate and environment may have elements that are perceived as threats or act as annoyances to the learner. There are a number of simple solutions for creating a brain-compatible and body-compatible classroom.

Let the Sun Shine In

Consider how you are using natural light in the classroom. The sun provides a full spectrum of light and can enhance general health (Hathaway, Hargreaves, Thompson, & Novitsky, 1992). For students who are able to spend a lot of time out of doors, the quality of indoor lighting may not be a critical factor. But as more children are spending a majority of time indoors, more frequent exposure to natural light could make a difference.

According to Geake (2009), "Another possibility for a school of the future involves changes to the physical classroom environment, particularly with lighting. . . . This suggests that the current widespread use of overhead neon strip lighting in school classrooms might need to be re-assessed" (p. 187). The following list of suggestions might be useful in making changes in the classroom:

- Make sure classroom windows are free of unnecessary curtains, blinds, or decorations.
- Poll students to find out which ones believe they actually learn better when sitting near the natural light. Some choice of where students sit can be taken into consideration.
- Rotate seating arrangements and ask students if they notice a difference in their ability to focus, stay awake, and read text.
- When appropriate and convenient, consider conducting part of the instruction in an outdoor setting.

Adaptations for Institutional Lighting

Traditional classrooms may not have been designed with natural lighting in mind. To reduce heating and cooling costs, some rooms may not even have any windows. Standard fluorescent light fixtures are common in many of today's classrooms. Some use ballasts and baffles to deflect and enhance the lighting, but many broadcast the limited spectrum of light directly. Flashing, blinking, vibrating, and buzzing often accompany the fluorescent light fixtures, and students may not even be aware of how these effects influence their learning. To lessen the effects of harsh lighting, consider the following:

- Turn selected banks of the fluorescent lights off during parts of the lessons. If more light is needed, enhance the lighting in the room using small lamps with incandescent bulbs.

- Several small bedside table lamps with 60 watt bulbs can be strategically placed in reading areas, study nooks, and work areas. These simple enhancements may be welcome additions for many students.

- The vibrational quality of the lighting might be noticeable to some students and may create difficulty when reading text. High-contrast print (black type on bright white paper) can appear to dance around, making it difficult to focus and causing eyestrain. In such cases, allow students to wear a billed hat or a visor to help shield their eyes from the annoying light.

- The Irlen Method® (http://irlen.com) is a research-based method using colored overlays and filters over printed pages to improve the brain's ability to process visual information. Have students try using a colored (yellow, blue, or pink) transparency cut into a bookmark-sized rectangle as an overlay when they read text.

Working in a Dull Roar

Background noise in a classroom is always present and inevitable. Heating and cooling systems cycle off and on. Light fixtures can hum and buzz. As more technology appears in classrooms, a dull roar can be detected from computer towers, monitors, projectors, and sound systems. The nature and volume of the noise can vary considerably and can turn from a mere distraction into a nuisance. Students with attention disorders may find the ambient noise a distraction. Students with sensory sensitivity may become distressed or hyperactive. Research indicates that chronic background noise can affect children's attentional systems, their ability to develop speech and language, comprehension of complex material, and academic achievement (Maxwell & Evans, n.d.).

Following are a few coping strategies for those students who are sensitive to the background noise:

- In some cases, providing a soothing sound ("white noise" such as soft music, water, ocean sounds, and such) may mask some of the multiple types of background noises and promote calmness and relaxation.

- During student work times, foam earplugs can help reduce the background noise while still allowing a teacher's voice to be heard for instructions. We recommend the kind that are attached with a cord so that students can drape them around their necks when not in use. Use a sticky file folder label folded in half as a nametag.

- During independent work times, some students may work better with music on. Make sure that the volume is reasonable. If students are productive, don't question the type of music they are listening to.

- Students can wear old padded headphones from a listening station when they are working at a learning center. They don't have to be plugged into anything.

Air Affair

Indoor air quality in classrooms can be adversely affected in three main ways. First, the materials used in the construction of the building, including carpeting, paint, and furniture, may still emit volatile organic compounds (VOCs). Chemicals such as formaldehyde and acetone are not only carcinogens, but may also cause headaches, respiratory problems, eye irritations, and nausea. Second, bacteria and mold can be present inside classrooms and cause allergic reactions for some students. Third, the indoor air may have a higher concentration of carbon dioxide due to an inadequate ventilation system. This can cause drowsiness (Shaughnessy, Haverinen-Shaughnessy, Nevalainen, & Moschandreas, 2006). The following ideas are provided so that air quality can be maintained:

- Be a detective and seek out more information about the construction materials used in your classroom. Portable buildings and new carpet are often culprits.

- Be an advocate for routine mold checks in heating and air conditioning systems.

- Find ways to keep air circulating; open windows and doors when possible, and use fans.

All of the conditions affecting indoor air quality may also produce aromas that are unpleasant and distracting. Experiment with ways to improve how the classroom smells, but be sensitive to students with allergies. Here are a few suggestions to improve air freshness:

- A drop of a natural essential oil (lavender, rose, sweet orange) on a cotton ball or tissue before students enter the room can give a hint of an interesting aroma.

- When allowed, many teachers have used diffusers to keep a pleasant scent in the classroom.

- Keep clutter under control. Mold, spiders, dust mites, and rodents may be present in areas where there are boxes of books or paper, art materials, and food or cooking supplies. Clutter can be distracting visually as well as affect air quality and smell.

Basic Needs

The best differentiated strategies can be wasted if students' basic needs aren't met first. When a student is hungry, thirsty, tired, or in need of movement, the survival mode kicks into gear and hijacks the brain's attention. Psychologist Abraham Maslow proposed a hierarchy of human basic needs, which suggests that when one's fundamental physiological, health, and safety needs aren't met, it will be virtually impossible to move toward higher-level functions. In a brain-compatible classroom, teachers must attend to cognitive growth, but they must identify and address students' basic needs and their emotional well-being in order to ensure successful learning.

Hungry, Hungry Students

Science journalist Judith Horstman (2009) reports on the state of the body when hungry:

> With your blood sugar plummeting and your serotonin running on empty, you're having trouble concentrating and your brain is getting cranky. . . . We need to eat to get the fuel (glucose) and building blocks (essential amino acids) to keep us not only alive but on an even emotional keel. (p. 72)

Many students may need a little sustenance in order to keep going. (Of course, there may be limitations about providing food items for students in the classroom, so be sure to investigate any school or district policies before acting on any of the following suggestions.) Small steps one can take to address the hunger issue are:

- ◆ Consider storing individually wrapped snacks in a plastic tub with a lid to hand out when a student needs a little pick-me-up: granola bars (without peanuts), raisins, dried fruit, crackers, and so on.

- ◆ Be an advocate for students who qualify for free and reduced-price breakfast and lunch programs. Many parents don't apply for the assistance out of shame or other such reasons. Make sure students take advantage of the program.

To address the issue of hungry kids in the afternoon, several elementary schools have found success by switching the lunch recess time and the lunch eating time. This can be a simple solution for kids who usually rush through their lunches to get ready for the recess time and then feel hungry in the afternoon. When kids play first, they come in and really eat their lunch meals. Another option also involves a schoolwide commitment. Some schools are providing a timetable that allows for chunks of learning approximately ninety to one hundred minutes and then physical activity and nutritious snacks to get more glucose and oxygen to the brain in a timely manner.

Hydration Station

When first promoted, many "brain-based" classrooms emphasized the need for students to have proper hydration to maximize learning. Common sense tells us that insisting every student have his or her own water bottle at the desk isn't necessary and may actually cause a distraction. However, many children may not be getting adequate water intake in the course of the day. Hydration helps maintain appropriate circulation and blood pressure, transports nutrients throughout the body, facilitates the transfer of neurotransmitters, and may even help the lungs be more efficient in oxygen intake (Horstman, 2009; Sousa, 2006). Whenever a student complains about a headache or not feeling good, a drink of water may be a simple solution. Some suggestions you might consider regarding students and hydration:

- ◆ Make sure that opportunities to get drinks of water are frequent and that water is easily accessible.

- Choose your battles. For some students, getting up to get a drink provides a quick movement opportunity as well, sending more oxygen and glucose to the brain and lowering the levels of cortisol and stress.

- Teach children about the importance of regular water intake and the possible perils of carbonated and caffeinated beverages.

Wake Up, Little Susie, Wake Up!

Author David Sousa refers to the time after lunch as the "black hole of learning." Perhaps you have noticed certain times of the day when students get particularly sluggish. Each of us has a personal and slightly different body clock. This "inner biological pacemaker" (Horstman, 2009, p. 8) regulates body cycles and schedules of sleeping and waking. These circadian rhythms can shift as students get older. Some schools are experimenting with delayed starting times at the secondary level. In addition, when sitting for long periods of time, blood settles into the lower extremities and can actually lead to fatigue. There are several easy ways to get kids to wake up and be more alert:

- Have students stand up by their seats and activate their calf muscles by bouncing up on their toes, for example. When pumped up, these muscles can act like a second heart and help circulate blood up from the lower extremities.

- Have students slowly roll their heads around to stretch and loosen up their tight neck muscles. These muscles can constrict blood flow to the brain and can cause sleepiness. Shoulder rolls and arm stretches can release tension in the area.

- Use a movement strategy when processing new information or reviewing (see the following section, and Brain Gym International at www.braingym.org).

Move to Improve

Frequent opportunities to move around while learning may improve all students' general health and will be particularly welcomed by kinesthetic learners. Two recent studies at the University of Illinois show that regular exercise can actually bulk up the basal ganglia and hippocampi in children's brains (Reynolds, 2010). These areas are associated with attention, complex memory, and executive function. Following are strategies that teachers can use to encourage movement:

- Orchestrate ways for students to walk and talk with a partner as they review or discuss new learning.

- Design hand jives or gestures to help students remember key points or a pattern of information.

- Have students practice math facts, spelling, algorithms, and such while jumping rope, bouncing a ball, Hula-Hooping, and so on, and ask if they notice an improvement in memory.

Systems and Patterns

As described in chapter 1, when the brain builds networks of schemata, it is able to more quickly recognize similar patterns found in new situations. The brain is constantly seeking patterns in the environment and linking the new information to stored preexisting networks. Judy Willis (2009), a neurologist and teacher, states, "The brain is designed to perceive and generate patterns, and it resists learning or even attending to information that does not have or fit a recognizable pattern" (p. 110). Consistent familiar patterns and organizational systems within the classroom can improve behavior and encourage independence. When students don't know what is going to happen next and what behaviors are expected, they can experience anticipatory anxiety. Posting a daily agenda that highlights the major tasks for the class can help students create a game plan and set personal goals. Designing clear procedures about all aspects of the classroom activities will allow students to focus on learning rather than worrying about what's going to happen and when (Willis, 2008).

Daily Agendas

When students enter the classroom, make sure that an agenda is posted so that, at a glance, students know what the game plan for the day is. See figure 2.1 for an example. Posted agendas should be brief and include colorful visuals and enough information to inform students about what will be done at the beginning, in the middle, and at the end of class. Remind students what materials they should have with them. For middle grades and high school students, provide a graphic or photo of any seating arrangements that might be needed for that class period. This is also a good time to post any homework that was previously assigned.

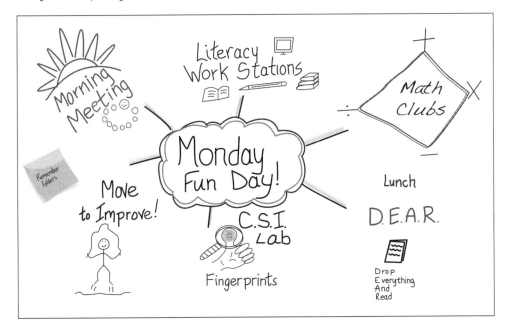

Figure 2.1: Example of a daily agenda.

A mind map sketched on a whiteboard or chart paper may be the easiest way to post the day's agenda. Use key words, simple graphics, or photos and icons, and indicate the order in which things will be done. Enhance the daily agenda with technology integration:

- Use SMART Notebook software to create a template and project the agenda on an interactive whiteboard. The agenda can be saved as a PDF document and posted on the class web page.

- If a data projector is used, create a scrolling slide show with pictures that show what the tasks for the day will be, seating arrangements or grouping changes, and what materials will be needed. (See fig. 2.2.)

- For an overhead projector, use a template agenda for each class. Fill in the specific details for the day using a water-based ink pen.

Power of Procedures

Classroom management skills will be a key to success when implementing differentiated instruction. Teachers who struggle to keep a classroom of students on task when everyone is assigned the exact same activity may be hesitant to try any differentiated strategies that involve regrouping or alternate assignments. Setting up classroom routines and patterns for all activities and tasks provides students with a system of orderliness. The brain is a pattern-seeking machine! When presented with a series of relevant, commonsense steps, and then provided opportunities to practice the pattern, the brain can store this as a program. Identify the behaviors expected during major tasks and activities that take place daily in the classroom. Design a set of procedures for each. Establish the steps, be consistent, and have students practice the procedure until it becomes a routine. Common tasks that require clear procedures are: arrival, dismissal, getting materials, turning in work, getting help, behavior during presentations, small-group work, what to do when finished, and cleanup.

Well-designed classroom procedures should address:

- Who the students may work with

- Where the students may work

- What behaviors are acceptable (talking levels, standing/sitting, and so forth)

- What materials the students may use

- When activities take place (appropriate times or how long)

Here is a sample arrival procedure:

1. Hang up your coat neatly.

2. Meet and greet other students with a friendly face.

3. Hand in your homework packet.

4. Check the daily agenda.

April 4th
On this day in history . . .

1968—Civil rights leader Dr. Martin Luther King Jr. was assassinated in Memphis, Tennessee.

1928—Poet and author Maya Angelou was born in St. Louis, Missouri.

Materials you will need today:

Core Class Agenda:

Review yesterday's *Romeo & Juliet* plot developments with a study buddy.

Meet with R & J Literature Circle: Continue reading aloud from page 60.

OYO (on your own)
Rewrite the famous balcony scene as a rap *or* in modern slang.

Where to begin:

Meet with your R & J study buddy and review yesterday's developments.

After 10 minutes, join with your R & J Lit Circle.

Figure 2.2: Example agenda, a scrolling slide show.

Routines and Rituals

Predictable routines create a feeling of safety and security. They can be comforting when students are going through stressful times. Some routines can be highly meaningful. Morning gatherings, weekly meetings, and monthly recognition rituals will help students learn what is valued, strengthen shared beliefs, and build a sense of inclusion. Consider when you might integrate a predictable routine, regular ritual, or celebration:

- Elementary classrooms may have daily rituals at the beginning of class—for example, morning meetings, circle time, Pledge of Allegiance. Birthdays might be recognized with an acknowledgment, special privileges, and a song.

- An "end of the week" meeting can be a time of recognition, appreciation statements, and reflection.

- An "end of unit" or a "learning celebration" ritual may be held to bring closure to a recent unit of study, celebrate what was learned, demonstrate new skills, or share products and performances.

Help! I Need Somebody!

In a differentiated classroom, as students work on their own, at centers, or in small groups, teachers must have clear procedures for how students can get help when needed (see fig. 2.3). Orchestrating a brain-compatible classroom includes creating procedures for students to use to find help on their own. When students know how to get help, they feel empowered. Create simple ways for students to get immediate help:

- Encourage students to ask other students for assistance and establish a clear "ask three before me" rule (of course, this doesn't apply to most testing situations). This rule prompts students to seek out a helper—three of them, if necessary!—before asking the teacher or another adult for help. Be consistent. As a student asks you for help, find out if he or she has already asked others. If not, insist he or she seeks out others first.

- Provide a stack of three colored plastic cups at centers, group tables, or lab stations. Green stacked on top means everything is going smoothly. Yellow placed on top means we have a slight problem and would like the teacher to check in with us soon. A red cup on top alerts the teacher that this group is at a roadblock and needs help right away.

- Response cards can be made by sticking a red and a green sticky note together or gluing red and green pieces of paper together. When the class is asked a question, students can hold up their response cards. Teachers can see at a glance which students might need help.

- In an elementary classroom, each student's name is on a clothespin. Have an "I Have a Question!" banner displayed at the front of the classroom. Students can place their name pin on the banner when they need some help.

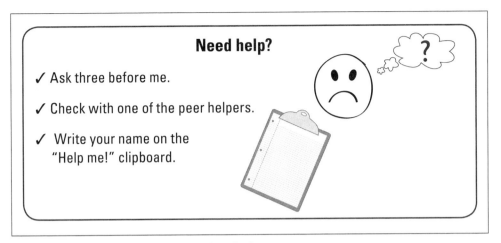

Figure 2.3: Procedure for obtaining help.

I'm Done, Now What?

When implementing varied instructional strategies in a classroom of diverse learners, it is inevitable that some students will finish before others. Or sometimes students have to wait for their turn at a station or for a computer. This is usually when behavior problems arise. Create procedures for students to know what they should be doing if they are done or waiting.

If a student is done or waiting, he or she could:

◆   Work on an anchor activity (see chapter 5)

◆   Check the agenda and prepare for what is next

◆   Work quietly on his or her own until the next transition

Stress Management

We've learned that a little stress and pressure can actually promote attention and learning. But what about those students who are experiencing stress, real or imagined, on a daily basis? It may not be stress that originates at school. Many children arrive at school worried about something going on at home. Employment and economic factors, family dynamics, and health issues may all play a part in creating stress in young children (Ratey, 2008). When students experience perceived threats or stress, their brains react with a reflexive response. Dealing with severe or prolonged stress can hamper natural learning:

> Stressed people don't do math very well. They don't process language very efficiently. They have poorer memories, both short and long forms. Stressed individuals do not generalize or adapt old pieces of information to new scenarios as well as non-stressed individuals. They can't concentrate. In almost every way it can be tested, chronic stress hurts our ability to learn. (Medina, 2008, p. 178)

Teachers can help students learn coping strategies and create environments to help alleviate stress.

Welcome Home

A few additions to your classroom decor may help students feel more relaxed and less anxious. Consider adding some homey touches to soften the institutional aspect of the classroom. However, avoid placing anything on display that is valuable, fragile, or may not be respected by students. Consider these suggestions for adding simple, interesting items that students will notice:

- Place an inexpensive welcome mat at the door.
- Add a living plant or routinely place fresh flowers in a small vase by the door or at your desk.
- Create a little display of a few items that represent you: a family photo or picture of your pet, a symbol of a sport you like, a postcard from a favorite vacation place, and/or a picture of you as a student at their age.
- Designate an area to routinely display beautiful things, such as an art print, a sculpture, a seashell, a pinecone, or a geode.

Emotional Temperature Reading

When students take a moment to be mindful of how they are feeling each day, they will build their personal reflection skills. When all students are gathered, ask them to quickly do an internal body scan, assessing their energy levels, emotional status, and physical health. Have students share this info with their groups or the class. Particularly ask if anyone is having a hard day.

Use a graphic chart or hand gestures to make a check-in more fun:

- Display a set of five emoticons (simple cartoon faces displaying various emotional states, see fig. 2.4), and ask students to rate how they feel by putting their fingers on the face that best represents their state.
- Students could indicate on a one-to-five gradient how they are feeling by holding up one to five fingers.
- Have older students simply give a thumbs-up or thumbs-down to indicate their general emotional and energy states.

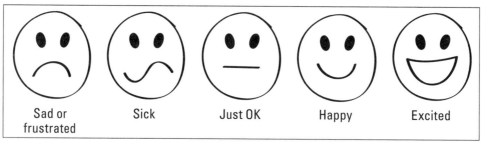

Figure 2.4: How are you feeling right now?

Take-Five Area

Encouraging students to notice when they are experiencing an upset or are getting stressed out helps them learn an important coping skill. Rather than always focusing on what consequences must be issued for poor behavior, provide a way for students to take action to calm themselves down—on their own—before they get too upset. Create a take-five area:

- Create a space within the classroom where students may go for five minutes with no questions asked. Designate a special chair (rocking chair, beanbag, office chair with a special cushion) in that area, and honor those students who show initiative and separate themselves from the class for a few minutes to calm down.

- Provide some visual aids to encourage relaxation and calmness: a lava lamp, an electronic photo frame displaying beautiful pictures, a beautiful shell or geode.

- With clear procedures for their use, provide some fidget toys, such as stress balls, bendy figures, or stretchy toys. Sometimes busy hands can help reduce stress.

Exercise

As mentioned previously, movement releases natural endorphins, helps the brain calm down, and lowers the levels of cortisol and adrenaline, thus relieving stress. When frustrated, students may benefit from some vigorous activity. Individuals may be assigned a task, or the whole class might get involved. Following are quick ideas for getting students up and moving around:

- Create a job for a student that would require a quick walk to the office to deliver a message.

- Ask a student to do a task that would involve a little work such as moving chairs, books, or tables.

- When the whole class is experiencing stress and anxiety, be willing to orchestrate a quick game of Simon Says.

Social Connections

Humans are social animals, and the need to feel included is a strong internal drive. Learning through imitation of peers, mentors, and adults has been going on for thousands of years, way before institutional education environments were created. Recent brain research involving mirror neurons is helping us understand how the brain is activated and begins processing when observing others do tasks. Learners may not have to go through extensive trial and error when they can observe a group member go through an activity. We can, in fact, learn from others' mistakes.

Some basic social skills must be developed to ensure success within group activities. Three key skills for success are: listening without interrupting, taking turns, and sharing. Multiple experiences in group situations will help a student develop these key life skills (Rabin, 2010).

Inclusion

Just because a group of students is assigned the same teacher for a particular class, that does not mean that they feel a sense of inclusion. Developing a sense of belonging and camaraderie takes time. Purposeful activities can provide a way for students to get to know one another on a more personal level. The resulting feeling of inclusion will generate a sense of security and enhance the brain's ability to learn. Continually build a sense of inclusion using a variety of strategies:

◆ At the beginning of the year, create a "people hunt" activity so that students can discover unique traits about one another.

◆ Frequently use a "four corners" strategy to let students demonstrate their preferences about things such as favorite foods, music, and movies. (See chapter 5 for further details.)

◆ Orchestrate small-group activities that require everyone's participation. Tasks that involve solving a puzzle or a problem allow students to work together on something and experience trials and successes.

◆ Have students do a daily check-in with their groups to discover how they are feeling each day. Finding out that others experience your same anxieties and excitement creates a sense of inclusion.

Tribes

The Tribes® model, originally developed by Jeanne Gibbs, is a wonderful collection of tools to help create a sense of inclusion among a group of students and even the whole class. Tribes Learning Communities (TLCs) help students feel included and appreciated, build respect for all of their differences, and promote positive interactions among students. According to the Tribes website (http://tribes.com):

> Tribes is a step-by-step process to achieve specific learning goals. Four agreements are honored:
>
> - attentive listening
> - appreciation/no put downs
> - mutual respect, and
> - the right to pass
>
> Students learn a set of collaborative skills so they can work well together in long-term groups (tribes). The focus is on how to:
> - help each other work on tasks
> - set goals and solve problems
> - monitor and assess progress
> - celebrate achievements.

Students are set up into small family groups that become their base group. This *tribe* becomes the group of colleagues they can count on and lean on when they need help and support.

Partner Up!

Opportunities to work with multiple partners in various configurations will provide students with chances to build their social and cooperation skills. Create a variety of student pairings and assign activities or lessons to the partnered students to complete. The following are ways to connect with a partner for conversation:

- ◆ "Elbow" or "shoulder" partner can be the person sitting right next to the student. Frequently ask students to check in with their elbow partner.

- ◆ "Study buddies" might be assigned by the teacher. Two students who might be good partners for a particular subject or type of task would routinely work together.

- ◆ "Clock partners" is an easy way to create a set of multiple partners for each student. Teachers can preassign some of the "appointments," and students might select a few of their own partners. Frequent opportunities to work with the same partner create inclusion and build social skills.

 Clock Partners

Using a simple clock face, have students note twelve work partners, writing down a different student's name at each hour. Some appointments can be selected by the teacher, and others might be selected by students. At various times, the teacher might say, "For this next learning period, please work with your three o'clock partner." Students can have their appointment schedule (clock) displayed inside their notebooks or taped to their desks for easy reference.

Welcoming Digital Natives

Creating a welcoming, stimulating environment for digital natives may be a bit challenging. Look at what young people are doing when they are outside of the classroom. The world of technology allows all of us to be connected 24/7. Many of our "screenagers" are socially connected to others during most of their waking hours. They text, look up information, play games, view video clips, and listen to music as part of their everyday routines. They really don't know a life without being technologically connected.

When these students arrive at school, many of them complain about having to power down for their classes. Students are not only bored in many classrooms, but the anticipation of having to be disconnected from their network may actually trigger anxiety and frustration. With a few small adjustments, educators should be able to create an environment that helps the Net Generation learners feel relaxed, ready to engage, and most importantly, respected. Consider how the classroom may be designed with a 21st century learner in mind.

Seating Arrangement

Are the desks, tables, and chairs able to be arranged in ways that promote collaborative and independent work? Seating should be appropriate to the task at hand. Set up the desks or tables in three or four useful configurations, and make up a plan for each that can be posted or displayed on a screen. Students can practice moving the furniture to the various setups, so that when needed, the movement isn't chaotic. Post the day's seating plan when students arrive to alert them as to what type of task will be done first.

Net-Savvy Hook

When teaching English learners, it is extremely important to be culturally respectful to assure students that you understand who they are. We should do the same when working with digital natives. It is the teacher's responsibility to become, if not fluent, at least savvy to terminologies, trends, and technological advancements.

Can you hook your students' interest with a reference to technology or an activity that involves using tech tools? By making a reference to or including a digital learning opportunity, students will feel respected and interested in what's going to happen next. This could be as simple as having a morning message prompt written in "txt" spelling.

So that students don't feel that they must power down, teachers might create a way to use technology at the beginning of the lesson. Using student response clickers or their own cell phones, students can respond to a quick survey by texting their answers to review questions on previous learning. Before class, take time to locate and then show a YouTube or TeacherTube video related to what you are teaching. If TV is available, consider checking out news events, weather, and such. Even a primary classroom's morning circle could be enhanced with the graphics and information posted by the Weather Channel. For older students, display a suspicious website that may not have accurate information. Ask them to analyze the data and discuss how they might determine the integrity of the information.

Many schools have worked hard to make a variety of technology tools available to their students. However, many of these whiteboards, document cameras, and even laptops sit idle while students are asked to sit still and listen to a lecture or finish a routine task before they get to use the equipment. Does your classroom look like a 21st century classroom? The environment should reflect the type of learning that you expect students to be doing. Laptops, computers, iPads, cameras, projectors, and such should all be out and ready and expected to be part of the learning process. When digital natives arrive in the classroom, their brains should not have to power down to endure a lesson designed a hundred years ago. Instead, their brains should begin to power up with enthusiasm and anticipation.

Differentiation will be easiest to implement if the classroom environment is designed with the brain in mind. Attending to the physical environment, social connections, basic needs, systems and patterns, and students' stress levels will create a safe and secure climate and environment. Learning is maximized when the brain isn't dealing with perceived threats, social isolation, and confusion.

Orchestrating a brain-compatible environment may be one of the most important aspects of an educator's job:

> Brain-imaging studies are providing increasing evidence that stimulating learning environments may be responsible for more rapid and robust neuron development. . . . Maintaining a rich learning environment, of course, should be the goal of all schools, but the research implies that school experiences for children and adolescents may have a significant impact on an individual's brain development and eventual level of intelligence. (Sousa & Tomlinson, 2011, p. 33)

Keep in mind that the 21st century learner may have different needs, and consider how the environment can be used to draw in the digital natives.

Chapter Review

Physical Environment: Lights, noise, air quality, furniture arrangement, and over-all cleanliness may all contribute to how the brain perceives the learning environment.

- Adjust classroom lighting, *page 32*
- Minimize background/ambient noise, *page 33*
- De-clutter and clean up, *page 34*

Basic Needs: Hunger, thirst, fatigue, and movement needs must all be addressed to maximize students' brain function.

- Lunch-recess switch, *page 35*
- Hydration station, *page 35*
- Move to improve and boost energy, *page 36*

Systems and Patterns: Agendas, procedures, routines, and self-help strategies for independence need to be in place and practiced to reduce student stress and anxiety.

- Post daily agendas, *page 37*
- Design clear procedures, *page 38*
- Systems/activities for getting help, *page 40*

Stress Management: Managing one's emotions and developing coping skills will help students reduce their stress levels.

- Decorate to create a "welcome home" atmosphere, *page 42*
- Emotional temperature reading and daily check-in, *page 42*
- Create a take-five area, *page 43*

Social Connections: Building inclusion among students, developing social skills, and creating small base groups of students will create a climate conducive for learning.

- Orchestrate daily inclusion activities, *page 44*
- Establish base groups of students (tribes), *page 44*

- Assign study buddies and small groups, *page 45*

Classrooms for 21st Century Learners: Designing classroom environments that respect how digital learners' brains work keeps them from feeling that they have to power down when at school.

- Create flexible seating plans that lend themselves to a variety of collaboration opportunities, *page 46*

- Use tech-savvy references and tools to hook students' interests, *page 46*

- Whatever technology tools are available should be out and used frequently within the lesson, *page 46*

Engaging, Exciting, and Energizing the Learner

One principle that propels the digital revolution is our brain's craving for new, exciting, and different experiences. . . . Whether excessive or subtle, the instinct to pursue new and exciting experiences frequently drives our behavior.

—Gary Small

One of the more difficult aspects of teaching can be getting students' attention so that they attend to and ultimately learn the lesson and task. Knowing what types of stimuli will engage the brain can help teachers plan strategies to get their students' attention. When not involved in survival issues, such as reacting to perceived threats, our brains are most sensitive to novelty and changes that arouse curiosity. New and unexpected sensory input in the environment will immediately get our brains' attention. Even slight changes in one's surroundings will create curiosity, and the brain will reorient toward the new information. Developing novel situations and using a variety of differentiated strategies can increase a teacher's chances of shifting students from disinterested to excited and energized!

Noted professor, author, and brain research interpreter Robert Sylwester often told teachers in his workshop sessions, regarding their students, "It's not that they aren't paying attention. They're just not paying attention to you."

There are two main types of attention: goal-driven and stimulus-driven. When focused on a goal or task to be done, especially if it is meaningful and relevant, our brains are capable of ignoring many internal and external distractions and inhibiting sensory stimulation so that we can fully attend to the goal at hand. However, maintaining sustained focused attention has its limitations. Our brains also need downtime in order to process new learning. Depending on the age of the learner, the ability to maintain sustained focused attention may last between five and twenty minutes. However, stimulus-driven attention occurs when sensory input is detected that indicates a survival issue. Then our brains quickly abandon focus and redirect to the source of the possible danger or threat.

Other stimuli can capture our attention, too. Movement, colors, sounds, tastes, discrepant events, humorous situations, and puzzling occurrences can quickly trigger our curiosity and cause us to reorient to the new stimuli.

Using humor, novelty, mystery, challenge, choice, and a wide variety of technology, educators can develop a toolkit filled with possibilities to use on a daily basis.

Reticular Activating System— The Brain's "Gatekeeper"

The reticular activating system (RAS) is the first filter that data pass through when entering your brain. Located at the top of the spinal cord and reaching up to the midbrain area, the RAS is a very complex collection of neurons where sensory signals from the outside world and one's internal thoughts and feelings meet. The RAS filters information from external sources, bringing one focused item to your attention and sending it to your higher, thinking brain. Priority goes to changes in the environment—particularly changes that indicate a threat or danger. When threatening conditions do not exist, the RAS then focuses on changes or stimuli that arouse curiosity. Willis (2010) tells us:

> That is the key to the gate—the brain seeks input about the new, the unexpected, the colorful, musical, moving, aromatic sensations that are available when perceived or imagined threat is not blocking the way. When students are curious about something, they seek an explanation. This motivates them to persevere in seeking the information **they now WANT to learn, what they need to be taught**.

Getting students to engage requires more than just causing a shift in attention. Harvey Silver and Matthew Perini (2010) describe "the eight Cs of engagement." When students are engaged, they "begin taking ownership of learning activities. Their involvement shows concentration and effort to understand and complete the task. They do not simply follow directions but actively work to improve the quality of their performance" (Silver & Perini, 2010, p. 323). Silver and Perini suggest that there are eight motivators teachers might use to inspire engagement: competition, challenge, curiosity, controversy, choice, creativity, cooperation, and connections. We have incorporated these motivators into the following groupings for suggested strategies to promote student engagement:

- ◆ Novelty and humor
- ◆ Mini-challenges and competitions
- ◆ Activating prior knowledge and building curiosity
- ◆ Choice opportunities
- ◆ Digital hooks

Novelty and Humor

When sitting in a classroom that contains mainly predictable or repeated stimuli, students' brains lose interest and begin to seek novelty—from outside or from within. Sousa (2001) believes that children's brains have acclimated to the "rapidly changing, multimedia-based culture and the stresses from an ever-increasing pace of living," so students' brains respond more than ever "to the unique and different—what is called *novelty*" (p. 28). The reward center of the brain (triggering a dopamine release and a sense of satisfaction) is believed to be associated with our attention to novelty. When something unique, unusual, interesting, or challenging appears, our brain signals us to explore it in anticipation of a possible reward. Humor and opportunities to laugh can trigger an endorphin release. Using humor can create a positive classroom climate, get students' attention, relieve stress, and enhance retention (Sousa, 2006).

Love to Laugh

Normal human brains love to laugh! A wonderful sense of community develops when people laugh together. Physiologically, laughing can increase the flow of oxygenated blood to the brain, lower blood pressure, reduce stress, boost the immune system, and be a total body workout! There are three traditional theories about what our brains find as humorous (Brain, 2000):

1. **Incongruity**. In this case, "humor arises when logic and familiarity are replaced with things that don't normally go together" (Brain, 2000), when we anticipate one outcome and something else occurs. In science, this is referred to as a discrepant event. This type of humor is a terrific tool for increasing engagement in the classroom.

2. **Superiority**. In this case, we "laugh at jokes that focus on someone else's mistakes, stupidity, or misfortune" (Brain, 2000). This type of humor can get you in trouble in the classroom. It involves sarcasm, put-downs, and ridicule, and can create detachment rather than building inclusion.

3. **Relief**. When tension is high, a witty side comment or joke can provide a lighthearted mental break and relieve stress. In the classroom, you may want to initiate this type of tension reliever. If you aren't quick enough, the class clown will beat you to the punch on a regular basis.

What someone finds as funny is usually dependent on experience and age, and may be culturally specific. Young children may find bodily functions funny, and teens are more likely to laugh at sexual situations, innuendos, and any subject that adults might consider off-limits. More mature students will begin to find humor in subtle situations and will be willing to laugh about shared common predicaments and embarrassments (Brain, 2000).

There are a variety of ways to use appropriate humor and increase laughter and joyfulness in the classroom. For instance, you can start with a "joke-a-day" policy. Jokes can be provided by a teacher or shared by a willing student. Students can be asked to bring in jokes to be shared, with teacher approval. Good websites to investigate include:

- Aha! Jokes, School Jokes for Kids: www.ahajokes.com/school_jokes_for_kids .html

- South Salem Elementary, More Classroom Jokes: www.salem.k12.va.us/south /teacher/lounge/jokes2.htm

- Ducksters—Jokes for Kids: www.ducksters.com/jokesforkids

- Brownielocks—Jokes & Riddles: www.brownielocks.com/jokes.html

Visit **go.solution-tree.com/instruction** to access live links to the websites in this book.

Encourage students to create new words with unique definitions by blending two existing words together and inventing a new funny meaning. For example, according to UrbanDictionary.com, *pupkus* is "the moist residue left on a window after a dog presses its nose to it," and *telecrastination* is "the act of always letting the phone ring at least twice before you pick it up, even when you're only six inches away."

Start some classes with a funny hat, parts of a costume, or an interesting object. Ask students to guess why the prop is relevant to the upcoming lesson.

A Picture Is Worth . . .

It is estimated that around 75 percent of all information reaching the brain arrives through the visual system (Geake, 2009). Visual images are processed 60,000 times faster than written text (Burmark, 2002). Creating a visual-rich classroom will increase the likelihood of students orienting toward the images and paying attention. One way to do this is to use a single photo slide to generate interest and curiosity (see fig. 3.1), to serve as a prewriting prompt, or to jump-start a robust discussion about a topic or a literature selection. Good images can be found at:

- Joke-of-the-day.com: www.joke-of-the-day.com/pictures?

- Strange & Unusual Pictures: www.copyright-free-pictures.org.uk /strange-unusual-pictures

- Google Images search engine: www.images.google.com

- Pics4Learning.com: http://pics4learning.com

- WebQuest.org: www.webquest.org/freemedia.php

- Teacher Tap: http://eduscapes.com/tap/topic98.htm

What's Wrong With This Picture?

Optical illusions (see fig. 3.2) play tricks on the brain and are fun activities for students. A great source for optical illusions is the National Institute of Environmental Health Sciences KIDS' page (http://kids.niehs.nih.gov/illusion/illusions.htm). For more optical illusions and unusual pictures, try this site: www.sandeepkejriwal.com/illusions.htm.

Figure 3.1: Image example.

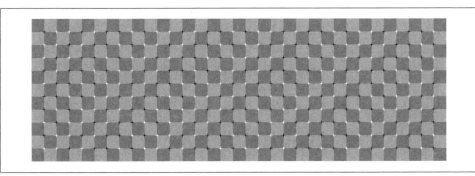

Figure 3.2: Optical illusion example.

R U Ready 4 SMS?

Have some fun with words, spelling, and language shortcuts. SMS (short message service) text is "essentially a simplified shorthand for communicating ideas that otherwise take a lot more words when spoken or written in formal English" (Carvin, 2006). Although teaching SMS text as a language at school may be a somewhat controversial practice, encouraging students to do some translations can generate some fun and excitement. Because messages have a limited number of characters and spaces (140, Twitter; 160, standard cell phones), text messaging is a real-world example of summarizing. Post the day's agenda or assignment in SMS text format to increase the chances of students noticing and paying attention. Encourage students to write a brief summary of a literature passage by allowing them to use SMS text.

Have a Wordle (www.wordle.net, see fig. 3.3, page 54) slide or graphic posted when students arrive. See if they can guess what the topic is for the day. Include several words that don't belong in the cluster and see if students can quickly discern which words are extra. This is a free web application for generating "word clouds" from text.

Figure 3.3: Wordle example.

Another free application for creating clever word clouds is Tagxedo (www.tagxedo .com). Tagxedo turns words from a book, website, letter, poem, vocabulary list, and so on into a visually stunning "tag cloud."

Funniest Videos

Students are living in a world filled with visual media. By the time a teen has graduated from high school, he or she may have spent twice as many hours in front of a TV screen than in classrooms (Burmark, 2002). A short video clip—especially one that is hysterically funny or ends with a surprise—can be a terrific hook to get students' attention and promote engagement. Short clips can help students focus quickly on the topic and make them more likely to give the upcoming lesson at least half a chance. Show students a mystery video clip and have them discuss with tablemates what the lesson is going to be about. Use a funny video clip to break the tension, relieve stress, and lighten the mood before beginning the lesson. (See chapter 5 for more on using multimedia to extend learning.)

Some great resources for video clips include:

◆ Source for free teaching videos: www.teachertube.com

◆ Source for funny video clips: www.youtube.com

◆ Another source for funny videos and more: www.funatico.com

Mini-Challenges and Competitions

In *A Handbook for the Art and Science of Teaching*, authors Robert J. Marzano and John L. Brown (2009) state that there are five factors that are key to student engagement: (1) high energy, (2) missing information, (3) the self-system (personal meaning and interest),

(4) mild pressure, and (5) mild controversy and competition. They also present the idea of "using games and inconsequential competition to promote engagement." According to Marzano and Brown (2009), "When students experience mild pressure while engaging in such activities as questioning, games, and competitions, they tend to focus their attention on key elements of the learning process" (p. 157).

Creating silly games and mini-competitions is a great way to attract students, but the emphasis needs to be on *inconsequential*. The ultimate results of the game shouldn't count toward a student's grade or a team's point balance. The purpose of the learning activity is to review or practice skills and content in a fun, interactive group situation. Some ways to alleviate students' possible preoccupation with winning include:

- Have the winning team or student get an immediate "inconsequential reward" such as getting to be dismissed first, or a new pencil, or a hall pass, or getting to have a classroom trophy displayed on his or her desk that is reused for each new competition.

- When giving points for tasks or right answers, make the amounts random and outrageous: two billion points or 3×107.

- Be consistent in your insistence that games and competitions are *for fun*. Play frequently with a variety of team configurations and always give chances for do-overs. Insist that students have a good time, play hard, and play fair, and everybody wins!

The contest questions or challenges may be directly related to the skills and content being studied, but that isn't a prerequisite for playing a fun game for a few minutes. Remember that for many students, a little pressure and competition may give them the energy needed to engage with the other students and begin to participate. A lighthearted, friendly game can be an amazing tool to develop inclusion and class camaraderie. There are a few easy games and mini-competitions that work well in a variety of grade levels:

- **Dollar words**. Give a numerical value to each letter of the alphabet: A = $.01, B = $.02, . . . Z = $.26. Determine the value of a word by adding up the amounts of the letters. Have each student determine his or her own name's worth. (All of a sudden, Ben [$.21] would rather be called "Benjamin" [$.68].) Then challenge the students to find "dollar" words—*fountain, swimmer, useless*—using a dictionary. The game can be played by individuals or in teams. Clever students can design a basic computer program to generate the words.

- **Sixty-second challenges**. In 2010, NBC premiered an exciting new game show called *Minute to Win It*. Contestants had to complete a series of simple tasks within a minute to win money. Looking almost like birthday party or summer camp games, most of the contests are easy enough to set up in a classroom with minimal expense and preparation. Go to the website (www.nbc.com/minute -to-win-it) for a list of the contests and the rules for each. Following are a couple of examples:

- Golf ball stack. To complete the game, three golf balls must be stacked freestanding one atop the other within the sixty-second time limit, and they must remain freestanding for three seconds.

- Pencil backflip. Unsharpened pencils are placed on the playing surface in increments of two, with all erasers facing the same direction. When the clock starts, the player picks up the first set of two pencils and places them on the back of his or her hand. The player must flip the pencils into the air then catch them together. The player adds two more pencils with each turn, building to a final set of twelve. The player cannot add the next set of two pencils until the previous set has been caught. To complete the game, the player must catch sets of two, four, six, eight, ten, and finally twelve pencils in succession within the sixty-second time limit.

- **TV game shows**. Many classic TV game shows can be made into exciting classroom competitions. For example, the classic *Jeopardy!* game can be formatted into PowerPoint slides. Once the template is made, new questions (answers) can be inserted to keep the game current throughout the year. Various websites share a version for free (http://be-a-gameshow-host.wikispaces.com /PowerPointTempates; http://office.microsoft.com/en-us/templates/quiz -show-TC010176929.aspx; http://facstaff.uww.edu/jonesd/games/index.html). Other game show formats that work well include *$25,000 Pyramid*, *Hollywood Squares*, and *Password*.

- **Internet searches**. Turn an online search into a mini-competition. Give student teams research tasks to be completed and time them. An easy format is a scavenger hunt; create a list of five facts to be found (or proven incorrect), and instruct students to cite their sources.

Activating Prior Knowledge and Building Curiosity

Another aspect of creating engagement is building a student's sense of curiosity about what is to be learned. Humans are drawn to new things; children, especially, are naturally curious. Pleasure can come from the joy of discovery.

The hippocampus appears to be always comparing new experiences to what is already known. When new information reaches the brain (words, sounds, images), the learner begins to mentally organize the information in working memory. When something novel, interesting, or unexpected is presented, the learner will try to hook the new information to prior knowledge by attending to patterns, details, and similarities. Neuroscientists believe that the hippocampus encodes new learning into long-term memories: "The hippocampus responds to rapidly changing here-and-now features by interweaving them with prior knowledge to create our ever-changing long-term memories" (Geake, 2009, pp. 60–61). Connecting the new mental representations to what is already known begins the integrated learning process, and the new knowledge or learned skill is filed in long-term memory along with feelings of confidence and a sense of accomplishment.

Vygotsky's Social Development Theory

Many aspects of our current quest to differentiate instruction are based on the constructivist theory of learning outlined by Russian psychologist Lev Vygotsky (1896–1934). His social development theory has three major components:

1. Social interaction plays a pivotal role in the process of cognitive development. Multiple interactions among students and with a teacher help facilitate understanding.

2. Learning is enhanced when a "more knowledgeable other" (MKO), such as a teacher, coach, capable peer, or technology source, is a part of the process.

3. The student's ability to solve a problem or perform a task must be within reach and be supported by an MKO. This is referred to as the "zone of proximal development" (ZPD). Learners will become bored and unmotivated if the task is not a stretch for them or if it seems unlikely they can accomplish the task. Students must be supported and challenged with tasks, concepts, and skills that are just a little beyond their current capabilities.

A student's prior knowledge must be assessed before the ZPD can be determined. Each student has a background of one-of-a-kind experiences that have wired his or her brain into a unique pattern. In a diverse inclusive classroom, instructional leaders must attend to differences in gender, language, ethnicity, culture, interests, aptitudes, and experiences in order to orchestrate appropriate learning tasks for all. One size will *not* fit all. *Fair* does not always mean *equal*. Using a wide variety of differentiated strategies, including multiple social interactions in partner and small-group work, students can move on to more complex material and skills when they have demonstrated mastery.

When a mystery has been created, curiosity ensues. Teachers can capitalize on the brain's natural curiosity by creating problems to solve, asking intriguing questions, and posing unique situations for students to consider. Students working with a growth mindset may be more likely to seek tasks that look challenging, are relatively unfamiliar, could result in a potential gain, and involve taking a risk. Students working with a fixed mindset may need more encouragement in a safe and secure environment to be willing to investigate, as they are likely to choose familiar tasks that are not as challenging to avoid risking a failure rather than trying new tasks. Frequently integrating a variety of clever and mysterious tasks may help build a student's interest in seeking answers and investigating possibilities. Try one of the following attention-getting suggestions:

- **Mystery box.** Hide something related to the content of the lesson or an item representing something that happened in a literature selection in the mystery box. A classic guessing game of "twenty questions" can be used as students try to discover what object is in the mystery box. Have a student tally the yes or no questions as they are asked.

- ◆ **What happens next?** Display photos of interesting situations, and have students guess what happens next. Explore and discuss possibilities. Great photos can be found online (for example, www.ahajokes.com or www.visualjokes.com/Clean /funny-clean-pictures.htm).

- ◆ **Can you believe this?** As students begin to conduct more research online, it is helpful to have them learn how to analyze photos and information for validity and accuracy. A great site to have students investigate is the Save the Pacific Northwest Tree Octopus (http://zapatopi.net/treeoctopus) site. Older students can explore the Belgium Doesn't Exist (http://zapatopi.net/belgium) site.

Choice Opportunities

As noted in chapter 1, all students develop clear preferences for certain kinds of learning and processing styles. A powerful motivator for engagement can be opportunities for students to choose what they learn, how they learn, and how they demonstrate mastery. Having choices immediately allows the learner to feel more in control, and feeling in control of one's learning experience contributes to self-confidence and empowerment.

Bloom's Taxonomy for Learning and Teaching

In preparing differentiated learning tasks to choose from, it can be helpful to review a common language for dimensions of knowledge, cognitive processes, and frameworks for writing educational objectives. Since 1956, a common tool used by educators has been Benjamin Bloom's *Taxonomy of Educational Objectives* (as described in Anderson & Krathwohl, 2001). The cognitive domain list of higher-order thinking skills has been the foundation of curriculum development and lesson design ever since. The simplified taxonomy chart started with the lowest levels of abilities and skills, *knowledge* and *comprehension*, and extended to the higher levels of thinking, *evaluation* and *synthesis*.

In 2001, Lorin Anderson and David Krathwohl (with Bloom's encouragement) led a team to revise the original taxonomy to update the language and make it more useful to educators. The revised taxonomy structure contains two important models for teachers:

1. Dimensions of knowledge: factual, conceptual, procedural, metacognitive (see table 3.1)

2. Taxonomy of cognitive processes: remember, understand, apply, analyze, evaluate, create (see table 3.2)

By matching the intended dimension of knowledge with a possible cognitive process level, teachers can write better learning objectives, and clarity of the educational objective is essential for designing and selecting the most effective instructional strategy. When integrating suggested activities and strategies from this book, first consider to which dimension of knowledge you are striving to teach. Is the content or concept to be learned factual, conceptual, procedural, or metacognitive? Then determine which cognitive processes (thinking levels) will be most beneficial to explore and learn the objective. Become particularly familiar with the process verbs associated with each dimension.

Table 3.1: Dimensions of Knowledge

Knowledge Dimension	Description of the Dimension	Type of Knowledge	Examples
Factual	The facts or content, often called "declarative knowledge," that students will need to know	• Terminology • Specific details • Facts	• Technical vocabulary • Symbols • Formulas
Conceptual	The attributes between and among the elements of a concept	• Classifications • Categories • Principles and generalizations • Theories, models, and structures	• Pythagorean theory • Law of supply and demand • Water cycle
Procedural	The methods of processing information or skills	• Subject-specific skills and techniques • Methods • Knowledge of when to use appropriate procedures	• How to paint • Scientific method • How to make a presentation
Metacognitive	Awareness of knowledge and ability to reflect on personal cognition	• Strategic knowledge • Appropriate context • Self-knowledge	• Knowing what skills are needed in situations • Awareness of one's own knowledge level

Source: Adapted from Anderson & Krathwohl, 2001.

Table 3.2: Taxonomy of Cognitive Processes

Category	Cognitive Processes	Definition	Alternative Verbs
Remember	• Recognize • Recall	Access to personal knowledge from long-term memory	• Identify • Retrieve
Understand	• Interpret • Summarize • Explain	Comprehension and meaning from spoken word, text, or graphics/symbols	• Paraphrase • Generalize • Conclude • Predict
Apply	• Execute • Implement	Procedures to use knowledge or skill	• Use • Carry out

continued →

Category	Cognitive Processes	Definition	Alternative Verbs
Analyze	• Differentiate • Organize • Attribute	Examination of component parts and the relationships between and among those parts as well as the complete structure	• Discriminate • Select • Distinguish • Determine
Evaluate	• Check • Critique	Using specific criteria to make judgments	• Test • Judge • Monitor • Detect
Create	• Generate • Plan • Produce	Creating a whole functional structure by rearranging and/or combining elements in a new pattern	• Hypothesize • Design • Construct • Invent

Source: Adapted from Anderson & Krathwohl, 2001.

Tasks and activities that focus on the lowest levels of each of these taxonomies (remembering factual knowledge) may not be as engaging as working at the higher levels of thinking (creating procedural knowledge and metacognition). Use the revised taxonomy to help you stretch your instructional strategies to more complex learning to intrigue and interest students.

The 21st century workforce requires fluency in a variety of thinking and processing skills. Tomorrow's careers will demand sophisticated skills that go beyond the basics. Designing student tasks and projects that emphasize the development and use of higher-order thinking abilities is more important than ever. Prensky (2010) speaks about teaching with verbs rather than nouns. In other words, focus on the thinking, doing, and processing skills rather than on the actual content and facts. Students are living in an era during which information is gathered just in time rather than just in case. Now, more than ever before, we must help students learn how to research, analyze, and problem solve. Information about anything is available to them instantaneously at any time and nearly anyplace.

Use your understanding of Bloom's taxonomy, learning preferences, and multiple intelligences to increase the variety of choices you offer students to hook their interest. Be sure to provide choice tasks that are equally interesting and rigorous. In this case, offering a choice enhances student engagement—getting students to begin the learning.

A or B?

Begin the lesson with a choice between two tasks. One activity should be a routine task, one that students are already familiar with. The other should involve something new and less familiar. When using choices to instigate student engagement, there should be no penalty or advantage regarding which activity one selects. They both should serve as a way to introduce students to the new material and hook them.

For example, when beginning a lesson on how worker bees use a "waggle dance" to communicate to the rest of their colony where the best source of pollen is located, activity choices could be:

A. Complete an online WebQuest to research the bee waggle dance using the NOVA Online "Tales from the Hive: Dances With Bees" site: www.pbs.org /wgbh/nova/bees/dances.html (OYO*). Guiding questions are provided by the teacher.

B. Work with another student to research the bee waggle dance using the science textbook and a copy of *Bees Dance and Whales Sing* by Margery Facklam (WWOOS*). Guiding questions are provided by the teacher.

*Students often respond to acronyms as they use them so much in their texting. They are novel, and the brain likes novel. Developing classroom acronyms can be a fun way of clarifying procedures. Acronyms such as OYO (on your own) and WWOOS (work with one other student) can be posted, and students will become familiar with them. They may even create some of their own for other situations.

Point of View

Begin a lesson with a discussion that encourages each student to assume a different role. Let students choose the perspective they would like to represent. A powerful tool for this exercise is Edward de Bono's Six Thinking Hats®. This parallel thinking tool guides participants to think critically about a topic from six unique points of view (represented by different-colored hats). According to the de Bono Group's website (www.debonogroup .com/six_thinking_hats.php), the Six Thinking Hats are:

- The White Hat calls for information known or needed. "The facts, just the facts."
- The Yellow Hat symbolizes brightness and optimism. Under this hat you explore the positives and probe for value and benefit.
- The Black Hat is judgment—the devil's advocate or why something may not work. Spot the difficulties and dangers; where things might go wrong. Probably the most powerful and useful of the Hats but a problem if overused.
- The Red Hat signifies feelings, hunches and intuition. When using this hat you can express emotions and feelings and share fears, likes, dislikes, loves, and hates.
- The Green Hat focuses on creativity; the possibilities, alternatives, and new ideas. It's an opportunity to express new concepts and new perceptions.

- The Blue Hat is used to manage the thinking process. It's the control mechanism that ensures the Six Thinking Hats guidelines are observed.

Pose an intriguing scenario or proposal to six students, such as "The FDA is considering approving a genetically engineered Atlantic salmon that can grow twice as fast as normal. Why might this be a positive event, or why might it have a potentially negative effect?" Each student is assigned to a hat and must participate in a rigorous discussion by only commenting from his or her assigned point of view.

Choose Your Own Assignment

For many students, having a chance to design their own inquiries, tasks, and assignments will really foster engagement. As they have already conducted research and worked on investigations that were designed by the teacher, they have the necessary prior experiences to make their own proposals. Marzano (2007) states that students should be given opportunities to move beyond basic levels of understanding and engage in tasks that require them to experiment with new knowledge and test hypotheses.

Create a proposal template that students may use; an example is shown in figure 3.4. Allowing students to participate in the task design will provide motivation and engagement.

Student Proposal for "Choose Your Own Assignment"

State what the particular problem, concept, decision, or experiment is that you would like to investigate and examine (related to a current curriculum study).

Write the proposal starting with a process verb (design, create, illustrate, persuade, experiment, analyze, evaluate, compare, and so on).

- Include your time line and expected scope of the task. (How big will the project be? How much time will you need?)

- Describe what the expected outcome should look like. (How will you know that you are finished?)

- Describe how you will show what you know. (Will you create a product or a performance?)

Figure 3.4: Student proposal template.

Digital Hooks

A variety of technology devices in the classroom can be a terrific asset when trying to generate and maintain students' attention. Kids are already multimedia savvy, and educators may miss the boat if they neglect to integrate new technology that can engage students' attention and satisfy their need for instant gratification. Willis (2006) states, "Now, with technology at hand or soon to be, educators and curriculum designers can captivate students through manipulation of sight and sound to stimulate their senses and to provide the feedback teachers need to keep student attention high" (p. 52). Digital hooks can be chunked into four main categories:

1. **Engagement**. Technology that creates interest and grabs students' attention with sight, sound, and interaction possibilities

2. **Differentiation**. Technology and computer programs that can differentiate lessons to enhance rehearsal and practice (keeping students within their zones of proximal development)

3. **Networking and research**. Technology and Internet applications that allow students to interact with the world and have instant access to information

4. **Assessment and feedback**. Technology and programs that provide students and teachers with instant feedback regarding the learning and interest level of students

The greatest inequities within classrooms today may be access to and use of technology. In Santa Cruz, California, a bedroom community to the Silicon Valley, one district has borrowed funds and purchased SMART Boards for every elementary classroom. At a neighboring middle school in a different district, a teacher has been conducting fundraising for over a year to buy her classroom the school's first SMART Board. Teachers should be advocates for increased technology resources (and appropriate training) for their classrooms.

Student Response Systems

Student response systems provide educators with the ability to actively engage students—even the shy or usually nonparticipating students—and easily assess student achievement. Students use small remote-type devices called "clickers" to communicate their answers and selections to the teacher. Student responses can be anonymous to take a class survey or specific to the students to assess current mastery. If a student response system is available in your classroom, consider starting lessons in the following ways:

- How are you feeling today?

    1. Upset and frustrated

    2. Tired

    3. Just OK; I showed up!

    4. Pretty good

    5. Feeling great!

- Regarding homework:

    a. I'm completely finished.

    b. I'm almost finished and could use a little time.

    c.   I've just started, not close to being done.

    d.   My dog ate it.

◆   Regarding your current understanding of _____:

    a.   I'm ready for the test; I've got it!

    b.   I need a little more practice and time.

    c.   I'm lost. Help!

Teachers who do not have access to clickers have found another way to get students' opinions and responses: have students use their cell phones to text in their answers or opinions. The responses are then shown on the teacher's PowerPoint display (with Internet connectivity) or on a SMART Board. There are a few free programs available for classroom teachers, such as Poll Everywhere (www.polleverywhere.com), that allow for this process.

Interactive Whiteboards

An interactive whiteboard is another great tool to engage students. It connects to a computer, and whatever is shown on the computer's desktop can be presented on the whiteboard. Interactive whiteboards also have recording capabilities, allowing a teacher to record and post an entire lesson. Software allows students to interact by touching and dragging information on the board. Board work has never been so fun! (Visit www.prometheanworld.com or http://smarttech.com for more information.)

Field Links and Simulations

Another way to hook students' attention and invite engagement is to use existing technology and classroom Internet connections to communicate with someone in the field of study. Local universities and laboratories may be a good place to start. Here are a few resources:

◆   NASA Quest offers the scientific process via online interactive explorations (http://quest.nasa.gov).

◆   University of Delaware marine scientists communicate with students from their latest research expeditions via On-Line Expeditions (www.ceoe.udel.edu /expeditions/index.html).

◆   Edutopia offers online adventures via virtual field trips (www.edutopia.org /virtual-field-trips).

◆   Students can become "eco-heroes" by participating in "green deeds" and posting them online daily (http://ecoheroes.me). They can follow others' efforts and may develop a following of their own.

Handhelds

Personal digital assistants (PDAs), smartphones, GPS devices, iPods, and iPads are finding their way into 21st century classrooms. In the beginning, handheld computers were used mainly by the teacher for data collection, developing student profiles, and record-keeping. As the technology has evolved into wireless connectivity, digital cameras, multi-media devices, and smartphones, now students can use the portable devices for a variety of instructional activities. In his book *Augmented Learning*, author and MIT professor Eric Klopfer (2008) states that mobile learning games and handheld devices foster many of the elements of authentic constructivist learning approaches and 21st century skills:

- Build communication skills and encourage social connections
- Create authentic and meaningful situations and contexts
- Connect learners to the real world with limitless boundaries
- Contain open-ended situations and multiple pathways for solutions
- Engage learners of all ages and backgrounds and are intrinsically motivating
- Provide immediate feedback to the learner

Many educators are creating a variety of ways to use handhelds in the classroom. While a few schools may be able to provide a mobile iPad classroom cart, some teachers have found tasks for students to complete in teams using just six mobile devices.

Using novelty, humor, visuals, mini-challenges, and new technologies may seem like a lot of scaffolding to do in order to inspire students' natural curiosity, but teachers must find practical ways to hook all learners and convince them to stick with the learning:

> Arguably, keeping students engaged is one of the most important considerations for the classroom teacher. Although it is probably not the job of classroom teachers to entertain students, it is the job of every classroom teacher to engage students. (Marzano, 2007, p. 98)

Chapter Review

Novelty and Humor: New and unexpected sensory input in the environment will immediately get our brains' attention. Developing novel situations in a classroom can enhance a student's likelihood of engaging. Using humor can create a positive classroom climate, get students' attention, relieve stress, and enhance retention.

- Love to laugh, *page 51*
- A picture is worth . . . , *page 52*
- SMS, *page 53*
- Funniest videos, *page 54*

Mini-Challenges and Competitions: If students can experience mild pressure while engaging in some fun activities, such as games and competitions, they tend to focus their attention on the learning process. Creating silly games and mini-competitions is a great way to attract students.

- Inconsequential rewards, *page 55*

- Sixty-second challenges, *page 55*
- TV game shows, *page 56*

Activating Prior Knowledge and Building Curiosity: Creating a hook to students' prior knowledge will help them create new learning and build new memories.

- Mystery box, *page 57*
- Revised Bloom's higher-order thinking skills, *page 58*
- Choice opportunities, *page 58*
- Point of view, *page 61*

Digital Hooks: Using a variety of technology devices in the classroom can be a terrific asset when trying to generate and maintain students' attention and engagement.

- Student response systems, *page 63*
- Interactive whiteboards, *page 64*
- Field links and online simulations, *page 64*
- Handhelds, *page 64*

Exploring the Learning

To take advantage of their engaged state of mind, students should have opportunities to interact with the information they need to learn. The goal is for them to actively discover, interpret, analyze, process, practice, and discuss the information so it will move beyond working memory and be processed in the frontal lobe regions devoted to executive function.

—*Judy Willis*

The five senses keep the body safe. The brain is constantly scanning the environment for interesting, novel, relevant things to pay attention to and ignoring everything else. In the previous chapter, we examined ways to engage learners, capturing their interest and attention so that they may participate in the learning process.

Once attention has been garnered, the information is moved to short-term, working memory. It doesn't have a very long shelf life there (perhaps seventeen to twenty seconds [Wolfe, 2001]), and if the learner is not actively involved in some task, the interest will wane quickly. Teachers are challenged with designing numerous rehearsal tasks that cause students to interact with a particular content or skill until it can move to long-term memory. It is during these rehearsal tasks that students explore and develop concepts and skills that will create lasting memory. With multiple interactions, the pathways that receive more use become stronger, smoother, and more efficient.

Classrooms are filled with diverse learners who come in with different readiness levels, interests, and learning profiles. Thus, "got it" moments vary. Some learners may need up to twenty-four practices to get to 80 percent mastery, but others may require only a few (Marzano, Pickering, & Pollock, 2001).

Rote and Elaborative Rehearsal

There are two types of rehearsal: rote and elaborative. Rote rehearsal is a mechanical memorization process that is used for things that require repetition and practice such as multiplication tables or capital cities. Basically, it's drill. Rote rehearsal develops repetition priming. Repetition priming is a memory that is developed through repetition and requires less neural activity over time (Wig, Grafton, Demos, & Kelley, 2005). In other words, the more you repeat something, the less the brain has to work to recall it.

Elaborative rehearsal, on the other hand, is processing information in a variety of ways, such as connecting ideas, finding patterns, debating, and comparing. We don't usually practice only one way, as it becomes boring. The more ways we practice something, the more memory pathways are created. These practices are sometimes referred to as "active processing." Practicing through social interaction, use of graphic organizers, or summarizing and note taking are ways of interacting with content and concepts that are engaging and provide multiple rehearsals. Developing elaborative rehearsal strategies is really the meat and potatoes of differentiation.

Best Practices for Active Processing

We are fortunate to have strategies proven to increase student achievement. The following nine strategies were researched in the 1990s at the McREL labs and were originally shared in *Classroom Instruction That Works* (Marzano et al., 2001). These best practices align with how the brain operates. They also provide rehearsal opportunities (active processing) that respect visual, auditory, and tactile/kinesthetic learners and provide settings for the various multiple intelligences.

Comparing and Contrasting

Identifying characteristics or attributes of a concept is a critical thinking skill. Comparing two concepts for similar or different attributes takes the thinking one step higher. Teachers can help students develop a deeper understanding of the concept through this process.

Brain bit: The brain seeks patterns, connections, and relationships between and among known information and new information. Compare-and-contrast strategies satisfy the brain's need to identify those similarities and differences.

In the classroom: Students need to be provided with opportunities to further examine content and topics through the analysis of similar attributes and differences. Grouping similar items or ideas and discerning any discrepancies between and among others are higher-order thinking skills. Teachers can model and then allow students to use Venn diagrams, cross-classification charts, analogies, and metaphors to connect new learning and ideas to past learning or experiences. Such exercises identify the key attributes of particular ideas and help in the memory process.

Summarizing and Note Taking

Recording information through taking notes either in written or graphic form is a key skill. It is more of a thinking process for students to identify key and supporting information and discard unnecessary details than to simply copy from what the teacher has identified on the SMART Board, overhead, or whiteboard.

Brain bit: The brain pays attention to what is meaningful and relevant and deletes what is not.

In the classroom: Picking out key points and restating critical elements when taking notes are important learning skills. Copying from the board or a textbook is a mechanical process, not a thinking process. Students need to be able to identify what is essential and what is supporting information. Tools such as graphic organizers and frames of reference can be used to accomplish this task.

Reinforcing Effort and Providing Recognition

Students often attribute success in school to fixed intelligence (whether they consider themselves smart or not) or luck. They often don't recognize effort as a key contributor to personal success. Teachers who help students see that effort is necessary and foster methods of self-reflection and metacognition help students develop a sense of self-efficacy.

Brain bit: Positive emotions garnered through relevant and useful feedback satisfy the brain and cause the release of dopamine, a feel-good neurotransmitter.

In the classroom: Students need to learn that effort—more than luck or even ability—results in success. Specific, timely feedback can increase students' self-esteem and their knowledge of what they are doing well and what the next steps might be. Grades without specific feedback will not help students move forward. Metacognition, reflection on performance and results, and goal setting are all valuable processes to help students recognize the relationship between success and effort and perseverance.

Assigning Homework and Practice

The issue of homework is often a contentious issue for students, teachers, and parents. Homework should be assigned to increase skill or develop concepts and reinforce new learning. Often it ends up being busywork. Teachers can extend what was presented in class in a homework assignment. For example, students who are studying percentages might be asked to find a bargain in the newspaper based on percentage reduction and calculate the cost of five items.

Brain bit: If you don't use it, you lose it. Perfect practice makes perfect. Opportunities for the brain to connect and strengthen neural pathways are offered through multiple rehearsals.

In the classroom: Homework is an opportunity for students to practice beyond the classroom in different and novel ways, not just "more of the same." Parents should support the students in completing homework independently at a designated place and time. The purpose for homework, including policies, outcomes, and feedback, should be clear to all who are involved. Homework also is a check for understanding and provides data to the teacher to help him or her regroup, reteach, or differentiate.

Generating Nonlinguistic Representations

The written word does not resonate with all learners. Many need visual or physical representation to imprint information in a stronger neural network. Graphics, illustrations, and models as well as drama and role playing can be beneficial for the memory process.

Brain bit: Visual stimuli are recalled with 90 percent accuracy (Wolfe, 2001). Tactile and kinesthetic learners usually appreciate more hands-on and whole-body activities. That way, more areas of the brain are involved; motor/sensory, occipital, and temporal areas are engaged.

In the classroom: In creating nonlinguistic representations, teachers can allow students the opportunity to flex their multiple intelligences. Digital photography, graphic designs, and student-designed websites are examples of nonlinguistic ways for digital natives to build their understanding in their first language.

Using Cooperative Learning

This strategy not only impacts student achievement but also the positive attitudes of students and the growth of social skills, tolerance, and psychological well-being (Johnson, Johnson, & Holubec, 1998). Cooperative group learning differs from group work by how the groups and tasks are structured.

Brain bit: The brain is social and needs positive interactions with others.

In the classroom: Over thirty years of research studies have proven that cooperative group learning increases learning and employs higher-order thinking skills. It also encourages the development of appropriate social skills. In the 21st century, cooperative learning may continue to broaden its definition as students are able to network with collaborative groups within a classroom, across the continent, and around the world.

Setting Objectives and Providing Feedback

When goals are set, the brain works both consciously and subconsciously toward the objective. Providing feedback regarding what is working well and what needs to be done helps the learner continue toward the goal, as he or she sees progress and is compelled to continue.

Brain bit: The brain responds to high challenge and clear targets. Specific feedback sets the bar for the next rehearsal, lowers stress levels, and increases self-efficacy.

In the classroom: Students should be encouraged to set personal goals, identify steps to achieve those goals, and monitor their progress. Feedback is essential: from the teacher, student to student, and self-reflection. Rubrics, checklists, and peer editing are useful tools.

Generating and Testing Hypotheses

When we ask students to draw conclusions related to new knowledge or skills, they consider all aspects of the information and use higher-order thinking. Making predictions also creates curiosity in the learner so that he or she is more engaged and connected to the learning.

Brain bit: The brain is curious and has an innate need to make sense and hypothesize with information it is learning.

In the classroom: Students should offer their hypotheses and rationales for situations and problems. Problem-based learning is a great way to encourage students to dig deeper into ideas.

Providing Questions, Cues, and Advance Organizers

Advance organizers, such as short readings, background lecturettes, or a graphic organizer with an overview, provide the brain with a contextual map for the new learning. Cues and questions also prime the learner for the new knowledge by accessing prior knowledge and experience.

Brain bit: The big picture helps the brain see where and how the pieces fit.

In the classroom: Prior to presenting new learning, teachers should encourage students to discuss what they know about the topic and any related information to set a context for the new learning and create curiosity and intrigue. This helps in preassessing the knowledge and skills (related to standards) that a student possesses and provides a context for the learning experience to come.

Using the Essential Nine Strategies

Teachers should employ these best practices to make the biggest impact on differentiated instruction. Several will be looked at more closely in this chapter.

Elaborative rehearsal is enhanced and accepted by learners when teachers use brain-based strategies to provide multiple methods for multiple rehearsals. The brain loves novelty, and using a variety of strategies that appeal to the multiple intelligences will provide interest and engagement and hopefully embed the learning in long-term memory.

Long-Term Memory

When sufficient rehearsal (rote or elaborative) has taken place, information, concepts, and skills move into long-term memory. This information is unconsciously filed in networks of association in the long-term memory, as we would be overwhelmed with too much information if it was all in short-term memory, where we only have seven memory spaces plus or minus two in short-term working memory.

John Sutton (2004) comments that information doesn't do well in cold storage. If never accessed or used, we lose it. In order to be able to access information from long-term memory and prevent it from being lost, it is important to retrieve the information now and then. It takes at least five to seven seconds to retrieve information from long-term memory as the brain must scan the files to find what is needed (Wolfe, 2001). Cyndi McDaniel (2003) states that numerous studies have shown that repetition has a positive effect on learning. Repetition with multiple retrievals increases memory. Thus, if concepts are crucial, it is important to access them multiple times to strengthen the neural pathways, increasing the ease of retrieval over time and also the ability to retain them.

Cooperative group learning is a powerful strategy used to rehearse and apply content and skills in a social way to help create long-term memory and increase higher-order thinking.

Cooperative Group Learning

Networking and collaborating with others are clearly skills that the Net Generation has been developing. Today, our students connect on Facebook, play multiuser games, text each other hundreds of times a day, and share information, music, and videos constantly. They form relationships and interact with each other efficiently, while perhaps never meeting face to face.

The brain is a social organ. It needs to communicate and interact to better understand and process new learning. The social aspect of learning in a positive, supportive environment increases the chances that learning takes place and is memorable, and the emotional impact of acceptance in a group is satisfying for the brain.

Cooperative group learning is a key strategy for the differentiated classroom; flexible grouping is necessary so that all students succeed and to accommodate the different rates of learning throughout a unit of study. Flexible groupings may occur randomly, the teacher can construct them based on personalities that are complimentary, or they may be organized by students' choice related to a topic or project.

Cooperative groups are generally heterogeneous and constructed with students differing by readiness, reading levels, or levels of thinking. When students are working in small heterogeneous cooperative groups, they are cross-pollinating ideas and capitalizing on the use of other high-impact strategies integrated into the group activity, such as using graphic organizers, taking notes, and identifying similarities and differences. Not only does cooperative group learning increase student achievement, but it also helps students develop social skills that they need to be successful in life. Research (Johnson & Johnson, 1991) shows that we can expect the following as results of the effective use of cooperative group learning:

- Greater self-esteem
- Greater student achievement
- Greater retention of material

- Increased social support
- Increased collaborative skills
- More positive attitudes toward school and teachers
- Higher levels of reasoning

Cooperative learning gives students a chance to explore new concepts and skills in a safe environment with opportunities for interests and preferences to emerge and flourish. Aural processing takes place, and vocabulary is used in context—the combination involves many levels of thinking.

Successful Group Work

The following five elements increase the chances that group interactions will result in student learning and students using their time together well:

1. **Positive interdependence**. The task is designed so that students feel that they need each other to complete it. Students understand the goal, and they are assigned roles, tasks, a task sequence, and the environment where the work is to be done. Each member knows his or her role and responsibility.

2. **Individual accountability**. Each member learns material, helps with and understands the assignment, and is responsible for the learning.

3. **Group processing**. Students have a discussion on the process of learning. A quick discussion is helpful for skill growth and development.

4. **Social/collaborative skills**. The teacher must be explicit about the skills of communication, leadership, trust, decision making, and conflict resolution.

5. **Face-to-face interaction**. This allows for the development of the skills of oral summarizing, giving and receiving explanations, debating, and elaborating.

Michael Doyle and David Straus (1976) suggest that gum is the content we give to the learners, and processing is chewing the gum. We should give less gum and more chewing time in classrooms, allowing many opportunities for students to interact in pairs and small groups to chew on information and ideas and make sense of them.

Teachers are sometimes concerned about allowing students to work together. However, the benefits of dialogue far outweigh the management concerns that can be dealt with in an expedient and positive way.

Dialogue allows students to:

- Clarify their thinking
- Develop oral language dexterity and patterns
- Develop vocabulary
- Expand concepts

Dialogue is also a wonderful assessment tool. As teachers are working the room and eavesdropping on students' discussions, they are learning who knows what and any misconceptions that are still lurking.

Teachers are sometimes reluctant to use cooperative group learning because of a variety of concerns. Table 4.1 provides examples of such concerns.

Table 4.1: Concerns and Solutions When Students Work in Groups

Concern	Solution
It takes too much time.	The time is well spent if students are clarifying their thinking and expanding their understanding.
Students are off task.	They need a clear expectation for the time they are working together and a realistic time frame. Use a timer.
One student does all the work, and the rest are social loafers.	This is less likely to happen if students are working with only one other person.

To deal with some of these concerns and avoid issues that can emerge with cooperative groups, have students work with partners for a while before getting into larger and more complicated groupings. Pairs are often more engaged because they only have one other person to interact with and plenty of work to do. There will likely be less conflict with only two people. Also, when students are later expected to work with everyone, they tend to feel more comfortable because they have prior experience with everyone in the classroom and have built connections and alliances.

Adding a variety of partner interactions will alleviate boredom. Random partners can be selected using techniques such as "point and go," during which teachers ask students to look at another student, point to him or her, and then move to have a conversation with that student. "Elbow" or "turn to" partners doesn't take a lot of time. For this technique, the teacher asks the students to discuss something with the student closest to their elbow or beside or behind them. Sometimes teachers use appointment cards to set up partner work in advance.

Moving to join up with partners is a brain-compatible activity as movement can send (within a minute) 15 percent more oxygen and glucose to the brain and can lower the cortisol level in the bloodstream (Sousa, 2011).

Think-Pair-Share

The strategy of think-pair-share (Lyman, 1981) increased students' test scores by 60 percent in a study in the United Kingdom (Black & Wiliam, 2009). This is such a simple technique with such a high payoff. If students are given a question and allowed to think about it, with sufficient wait time (for the brain to recall and sort out the details) and no pressure, more of them are likely to be engaged. Pairing with a partner to check out their thinking, debate, and clarify ideas provides a social aspect to the situation, which satisfies the brain and also continues to lower the risk of being wrong. Sharing with the larger group after clarification and rehearsal have taken place allows the auditory learners to benefit from the process and feel comfortable, but the activity is also beneficial to all learners. Students are using technology to tweet, blog, and email, but they also need the opportunity to interact face to face and develop the interpersonal skills needed for the 21st century.

Write-Pair-Share

This strategy works similarly to think-pair-share, but the "think" part is written. Some students need a chance to capture their thoughts and have something to refer to when they move to the next step of pairing. They can edit or refine their notes during the peer discussion. This allows the tactile learner to benefit from the process and feel comfortable, but the activity is also beneficial to all learners. Technology and social networks can be used for this activity.

Draw-Pair-Share

This strategy works similarly to write-pair-share, but the "think/write" part is drawn with pictures or symbols. Some students need a chance to capture their thoughts and have something to refer to when they move to the next step of pairing. They can edit or refine their illustrations during the peer discussion. This allows the visual learner to benefit from the process and feel comfortable, but the activity is beneficial to all learners. Using technology and programs such as Kidspiration (www.inspiration.com/Kidspiration) and Inspiration (www.inspiration.com) will enhance this strategy.

TIPS for Grouping

Collaboration is one of the key 21st century skills. Educators can embed the practice of this skill while helping students reach targeted standards in all subject areas by having them work in heterogeneous groups that model how the real world of business, industry, families, and organizations operates.

Table 4.2 (page 76) offers TIPS to help teachers consider the types and uses of grouping in the classroom. All of these configurations could and should be used throughout the day as students need interaction and a change of venue and state. Sometimes the groupings are meant to provide variety, and sometimes they are based on need.

Here Is . . . Where Is?

This strategy is a good way to process, rehearse, and review new information. It helps visual, auditory, and kinesthetic learners focus their attention. It provides social interaction, is physically engaging, and creates healthy, supportive competition.

Table 4.2: TIPS for Grouping

	Student Grouping	Strategy
Total	Instruction for the whole group at the same time	Delivery of new information New skills demonstrated Guest or expert Watching a video or DVD Using the jigsaw strategy Preassessment Reading a text
Independent	All students working independently on a variety of activities related to interest, readiness, or choice	Log or journal entry Preassessment Portfolio self-assessment and goal setting Independent study Taking notes and summarizing Reflection Quick writes and exit cards

Partners	Students have a processing partner, determined by:
	  Random selection (elbow, point and go, or other such method)
	  Teacher or student
	  Task or interest choice
		Reviewing homework
		Checking for understanding
		Processing information
		Peer editing and evaluation
		Researching/investigation
		Interest in similar task
		Brainstorming

Small groups	Groups determined by:
	  Similar needs for skill development
	  Cooperative groups
	  Structured by teacher or students
	  Random
	  Interest or task oriented
		Group projects
		Cooperative group learning assignments
		Portfolio conferences
		Group investigation
		Group brainstorming
		Group problem solving

Source: Adapted from Gregory & Kuzmich, 2004.

"Here is . . . Where is?" (adapted from Tilton, 1996) is a simple review strategy that can be used with any content or subject area. The teacher prepares cards with an answer to a question (Here is) and a new question (Where is?). One card will say "Start here." This strategy can be done as students sit in a circle. For students who need assistance, a partner may be assigned or a resource teacher may sit with them.

The process is as follows:

1. Distribute the cards among students randomly.

2. The student with the "Start here" card will begin the process by reading the first question aloud.

3. The participant who believes he or she is holding the correct answer reads it from the card (Here is . . .).

4. If a wrong answer is given, pause and review the question so that the students will check their cards again and the person with the correct answer will respond.

5. Once a student reads the correct answer, the game will resume with that student asking the question on his or her card.

6. This process continues until all the cards are read and the student who started finishes the chain.

7. Students exchange cards, and the game starts again.

The teacher may have three sets of cards for the same topic, including one more difficult or challenging and one less complex. Students are grouped so that they are at the level of appropriate challenge. Everyone is engaged in the same task but at his or her own level of readiness and understanding.

Figure 4.1 provides a math example. A blank template for this activity can be found on page 88. Visit **go.solution-tree.com/instruction** to download the reproducibles in this book.

Start here Here is 75% Where is? 50%	Here is .50 Where is? 25%
Here is .25 Where is? $\frac{7}{8}$	Here is .88 Where is? 30%
Here is .30 Where is? 60%	Here is .60 Where is? 66 $\frac{2}{3}$%
Here is $\frac{2}{3}$ Where is? 55%	Here is .55 Where is? 70%
Here is .70 Where is? 90%	Here is .90 Where is? $\frac{3}{4}$

Figure 4.1: Here is . . . Where is?: percentage and decimal equivalents.

Source: Concept adapted from Tilton, 1996.

Social Skills for Student Success

One of the main reasons that group work fails is that some students do not have the necessary social skills to work with one another. Many families have focused on these skills in their home, but others have not. Some students may have learned to say "please," "thank you," "pardon me," and "pleased to meet you" but may not have the prerequisite skills for successful group interactions. Explicitly teaching these skills is paramount to group work being successful. Following are some of the fundamental face-to-face social skills:

- Listening to others
- Taking turns
- Encouraging others
- Using positive statements
- Using quiet voices
- Participating equally
- Staying on task
- Asking for help
- Using polite language

The following are some skills for maintaining successful group process:

- Checking for understanding
- Asking for clarification
- Following directions
- Disagreeing agreeably
- Resolving conflicts
- Accepting differences
- Encouraging one another

It is crucial that educators teach the necessary social skills for optimal work in collaborative groups and to accomplish academic goals. To most effectively teach social skills, teachers need to help students understand the need for the skill; what the skill looks, sounds, and feels like; how to practice the skill; and how to reflect on the practice.

The Need for the Skill

Sometimes the need for a particular social skill clearly presents itself. For example, students are working in a group, and conflict occurs. The teacher intervenes and identifies the skill needed. The teacher stops the whole class and discusses the skill. Ideally, the teacher and students work together to analyze the situation and identify the skill that will help the group function better. Sometimes the teacher decides that a particular skill will be needed and highlights and models that skill. For example, in coming to consensus in a group activity, the teacher decides students need to focus on attentive listening so that they will be clear about what others are offering.

What the Skill Looks, Sounds, and Feels Like

Any learning target must be clear to the learner. To make a social skill clearer, the skill can be illustrated through a story, video, or current event. Students can role-play to get a sense of how the skill looks, sounds, and feels in action. Teachers can help students create a chart that details the characteristics of the skill. Thinking about feelings helps students with the skills of self-awareness and empathy. Table 4.3 is an example of a chart that describes "attentive listening." Students can generate these indicators as a class, contributing statements in their own verbiage so that, in group situations, the language is comfortable and familiar to use.

Table 4.3: Attribute Chart for Attentive Listening

Looks Like	Sounds Like	Feels Like
Eyes on the speaker Intent looks Leaning in Nodding	One voice at a time Regular voices	My ideas are important Satisfied that others hear me

Source: Adapted from Hill & Hancock, 1993.

Students can show that they understand the skill by drawing about it, role-playing a situation in which the skill is used appropriately, using puppets to demonstrate the skill, or writing about themselves or others using this skill in real-life situations.

How to Practice the Skill

Teachers need to design cooperative experiences and select a suitable social skill that could be practiced during the activity. For example, equal participation is an important skill to use when the group is trying to share opinions and come to an agreement. Attentive listening is important in activities in which everyone needs to be involved, feel included, and participate equally.

How to Reflect on the Practice

Due to lack of time at the end of a group activity, group processing is a step that is often omitted even though it is an essential component of cooperative group learning. Practicing social skills usually results in improvement over time, but processing after the practice will improve the skills even more as it raises students' consciousness of the skill and the outcome.

Processing should not take a large amount of time. A compliment to another member of the group to show appreciation is quick and positive. Perhaps a thumbs up, sideways, or down could be used to illustrate the level of success. Or students could rate themselves one through five, using their fingers to indicate how well they worked together for the task:

- 5 meaning "the best we could be"
- 4 meaning "a good job"
- 3 meaning "satisfactory"
- 2 meaning "needs improvement"—some evidence is there
- 1 meaning "we really have to review this skill and work on it"

Checklists and journal entries can also be used. Group processing encourages meta-cognition and helps students develop their skills in self-awareness and reflection.

If a student works on an assignment alone, he or she only has one perspective, opinion, and outcome. If students work in a group, they combine ideas, brainstorm, debate, summarize, challenge, and build on each other's thoughts. This taps into all levels of thinking, from recall to evaluation, and collaborative, critical, creative, and innovative thinking are being fostered as necessary skills for the 21st century.

Note Taking and Summarizing

Taking notes, answering questions, and completing a test do not address the diverse learning styles of students. There are many ways teachers can differentiate the way they share information and actively engage students. For instance, teachers can provide students with options for taking notes and reading texts, fulfilling the brain's need to organize, make sense of information, and select key ideas.

Strategies for Lectures

Often new information is delivered by the teacher in a stand-and-deliver mode. Lectures engage auditory learners, and with accompanying visuals, the lecture has more of an impact on all learners. However, the brain can't focus for long periods of time as it is used to looking for interesting or sensory stimuli (Wolfe & Sorgen, 1990). Making matters worse, digital natives who are used to flipping from screen to screen have a short attention span if the topic doesn't interest them.

It is more advantageous to use the lecturette method, during which the teacher gives a chunk of information and then allows the students to discuss it and write about it. This technique encompasses several changes of state that are more likely to keep the brain engaged and attentive. Lectures can actively engage students if they are given several opportunities to manipulate and work with the concept both alone and in small groups (Fitzgerald, 1996).

Today's classroom technologies provide numerous ways to disseminate content that can address individual student needs. Visuals are an essential component of any presentation/lecture. If using a PowerPoint or SMART Board presentation, for example, there are certain things the instructor should keep in mind:

- Use only key words.

- Emphasize important points by incorporating bullets or bold.

- Space things appropriately, not too much on a line.

- Limit the number of colors; too many make it too busy.

- Keep off to the side of the screen to avoid distracting or blocking.

- Use variety and novelty to eliminate monotony of the slides.

Some may find it helpful to have a note-taking template to fill out while attending a lecture. See page 89 for a blank template.

Graphic Organizers and Nonlinguistic Representations

Teachers can offer organizers to help students sort and classify information and to make note taking meaningful, creative, and useful. Students may use the organizers during a lecture or as a check for understanding after the lecture has concluded. Organizers help all learners extract key information from text, technology, or audiovisual sources. A McREL study (Marzano et al., 2001) suggests a 27 percentile gain in student learning by using nonlinguistic visual representations, which include the use of graphic organizers.

Graphic organizers have a number of characteristics that improve students' thinking and organizing skills. They help students make connections between and among pieces of information, making it easier to recall that information. They also help students to break information into manageable chunks. By chunking information, students are able to see the relationships among the separate pieces, and this is key to forming concepts, which leads to understanding.

Venn Diagrams

Some graphic organizers, like the Venn diagram, also facilitate the use of thinking skills such as compare and contrast. Free Venn diagram applications are available from SmartDraw (www.smartdraw.com/specials/venn.htm) and My Teacher Tools (www.myteachertools.com/venndiagram.php).

In figure 4.2 (page 82), students brainstorm what they know about each country, placing these attributes in the appropriate circle. Students then select the similar attributes and place them in the overlapping center of the Venn.

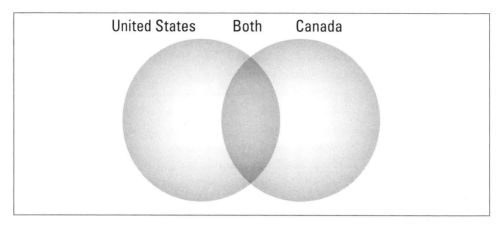

Figure 4.2: Venn diagram of the United States and Canada.

Students may begin by using a brainstorming chart to list all they know about the three wars, such as that in table 4.4. Teachers may also give students categories to consider such as reasons for involvement, length, types of warfare, and technical and medical advancements. Students will then transfer the information to the triple Venn.

Table 4.4: Brainstorming Chart

Criteria to Consider	Persian Gulf War	Iraq War	Vietnam War

Students can use the triple-circle Venn diagram to look at three ideas and find the similarities and differences. Figure 4.3 shows an example of a triple-circle Venn diagram exploring three wars: Persian Gulf War, Iraq War, and Vietnam War.

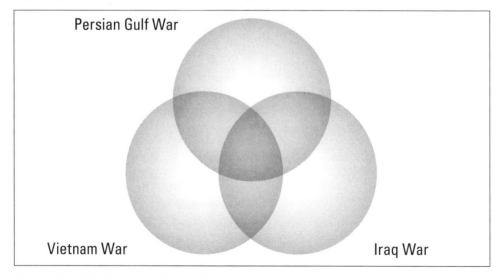

Figure 4.3: Triple-circle Venn diagram.

3-D Graphic Organizers

Sometimes the novelty of creating an organizer for recording information and key ideas is intriguing for the learner. Following are instructions for creating an eight-sided booklet that can provide space for recording eight vocabulary words or eight key concepts in a unit of study:

1. Take a rectangle and make a hot-dog fold.

2. Then fold it in half and then in half again. There should be eight sections.

3. Open up to the large rectangle, then make a hamburger fold.

4. Cut down the center, marking halfway down.

5. Open up and make the hot-dog fold again.

6. Then push toward the center to form a booklet with eight sides.

Foldable books and other 3-D graphic organizers add novelty to any lesson or processing activity. Find more examples of simple foldables online. Two terrific resources are: Tech-It & Take-It (www.vickiblackwell.com/makingbooks.html) and Dinah-Might Adventures (www.dinah.com/manipulatives.php).

Projects

Projects offer students a variety of ways to actively process content and skills. Students investigate a topic and create models or other applications. Projects can engage learners and help foster a deeper understanding at all levels of readiness or interest. Each project should meet certain criteria:

- Provides choices
- Is age appropriate so the students can do the assignment independently or collaboratively
- Rehearses content taught during the year
- Fits an established time line and is manageable and doable
- Has available resources
- Is assessed by an established assessment tool, often a rubric
- Provides opportunities for creativity and individuality
- Integrates several skills and concepts to deepen understanding

Purposes of Projects

Students rehearse and practice skills and content when working on projects. They also develop a variety of skills outside of the specific content. They learn how to:

- Plan their time
- Develop their research skills at various levels
- Make choices and take ownership and responsibility

- Work independently
- Develop self-directed learning skills
- Work at complex and abstract levels that match their skill level
- Manage time and materials

Projects are highly motivating and allow for in-depth work on interesting topics. Projects allow students to work at their own rate. They allow the brain to make connections and new neural pathways in a variety of ways. However, projects must be worth the time the learner will spend and be meaningful experiences, not just time fillers.

Principles of Projects

All projects need to be designed with the end in mind. That means that the project is designed based on clear learning goals, standards, and content objectives. Projects should be age appropriate and at the students' level so the work is interesting and challenging without being overwhelming.

The tic-tac-toe board shown in figure 4.4 provides suggestions for projects in each of the eight multiple intelligences. A board may be created to focus on one topic, concept, or skill (not just a fun activity). Students choose three in a row in any direction on their choice board. The personal selection in the center may be the student's choice from any other box that isn't in that row or a project that he or she suggests after checking with the teacher. The choice allows the student to work in an area of interest or preference and have a sense of control and autonomy, which lowers stress levels and helps create flow. The projects will be created using different levels of thinking: remember, understand, apply, analyze, evaluate, and create (see chapter 3).

Students' Choices

Being given choices creates a sense of independence and commitment to a task. Choice is a real motivator, and it's hard for a student to say, "I don't want to do this" if he or she chose it. Here is a list of many possibilities for students to peruse as they make a selection for a project. These help with the multiple rehearsals needed to truly understand new information and can also serve as assessments to gauge how the understanding is progressing:

- Write a poem.
- Create a rap, song, or ballad.
- Conduct an interview.
- Record the findings of an investigation.
- Create a vocabulary game.
- Create a *Jeopardy!* game.
- Illustrate a caricature.
- Develop an editorial cartoon.
- Design a collage.
- Create an advertisement.
- Draw a map.
- Discuss with a partner.
- Write a play.
- Create a model.
- List synonyms and antonyms.

Visual-Spatial	Bodily-Kinesthetic	Logical-Mathematical
Illustrate an event	Construct a model or representation	Organize a pattern
Draw a diagram	Pantomime the process	Develop a sequence or process
Create a mural, poster, or drawing	Create a tableau	Compose a rationale
Create a graphic organizer	Manipulate materials	Analyze a situation
Add color to . . .	Work through a simulation	Write a sequel
Compose a comic strip	Develop actions	Critically assess
Design a storyboard	Create a role-play scenario	Classify, rank, or compare
Create a collage with meaningful symbols		Analyze evidence
		Design a game or model
Musical-Rhythmic		**Intrapersonal**
Compose a rap, song, or ballad		Think about and plan
Create a jingle		Review or visualize
Write a poem	**Personal Selection**	Reflect on the character and express his or her feelings
Enhance a story or event with music		Predict how you would feel if . . .
Create rhymes		Keep track of . . . and comment on . . .
		Write in a journal
Verbal-Linguistic	**Naturalist**	**Interpersonal**
Write a report	Categorize objects or ideas	Work in pairs or a group
Create a play or essay	Look for ideas from nature	Discuss and come to a consensus
Write directions for . . .	Adapt materials to a new use	Solve problems together
Compose a poem or recitation	Connect ideas to nature	Survey or interview others
Listen to an audio or video tape, CD, or DVD	Examine materials to make generalizations	Dialogue about or debate an issue
Tell in your own words	Label and classify objects	Use cooperative groups to do a group task
Create a word web	Draw conclusions based on evidence	Project a character's point of view
	Make a prediction	

Figure 4.4: Choice board suggestions.

Source: Adapted from Gregory & Kuzmich, 2005.

- Write a critique.
- Develop a storyboard.
- Write your opinion.
- List the causes.

- Write directions.
- Give examples of.
- Debate an issue.
- Design a brochure.

The verbs of 21st century skills create additional choices to incorporate digital integration. Teachers should "... build on the foundational belief that new technologies are nothing more than tools that can be used to teach the kinds of old-school skills that have been important in the academic and social growth of all children, regardless of what generation they were born in" (Ferriter & Garry, 2010, p. 9). The choices for students should incorporate the use of digital tools when available:

- Create, write, and contribute to blogs or wikis.
- Participate in, create, and contribute to web conferences or webinars.
- Produce and edit digital photos and videos.
- Design, illustrate, and edit original digital graphic designs, cartoons, or ads.
- Record, edit, and produce podcasts, radio programs, or music.
- Research, annotate, and bookmark websites or search engines.
- Create, program, and publish websites or social network pages.

A rubric or check deck (see chapter 6) will clarify the expectations of the project.

By providing multiple ways of exploring and processing new content and skills, students engage more areas of the brain and create more neural pathways and memories.

Chapter Review

Memory Processing: Recognizing that students need multiple rehearsals to transfer information and skills to long-term memory

- Similarities and differences, *page 68*
- Summarizing and note taking, *page 68*
- Reinforcing effort and recognition, *page 69*
- Assigning homework and practice, *page 69*
- Nonlinguistic representations, *page 70*
- Cooperative group learning, *page 70*
- Setting objectives and providing feedback, *page 70*
- Generating and testing hypotheses, *page 71*
- Providing questions, cues, and advance organizers, *page 71*

Cooperative Group Learning: Recognizing that differentiated classrooms depend on the students being able to work with others in a cooperative way

- Positive interdependence, *page 73*

- Individual accountability, *page 73*
- Group processing, *page 73*
- Social skills—teaching, practice, and processing, *page 73*
- Face-to-face interaction, *page 73*
- Think-pair-share, draw-pair-share, write-pair-share, *page 74*
- Grouping: TIPS, *page 75*
- Here is . . . Where is?, *page 75*

Graphic Organizers: Using visual representations helps students organize and visualize information

- Venn diagrams, *page 81*
- 3-D graphic organizers, *page 83*

Projects: Providing students with choice and varying the opportunities to work in all areas of multiple intelligences and levels of thinking

- Tic-tac-toe, *page 84*
- Variety of performance projects/assessments, *page 84*
- Integrate digital technology into choices, *page 86*

Here is . . . Where is?

Here is **Start here** **Where is?**	**Here is** **Where is?**
Here is **Where is?**	**Here is** **Where is?**
Here is **Where is?**	**Here is** **Where is?**
Here is **Where is?**	**Here is** **Where is?**
Here is **Where is?**	**Here is** **Where is?**

Source: Concept adapted from Inclusion: A Fresh Look—Practical Strategies to Help All Students Succeed *by Linda Tilton.*

Note-Taking Template

Subject:	Date:

Headings	Key Points	Symbols, Illustrations

Summaries

Extending and Expanding Learning for Every Student

> The mission for a school of the future (or the present?) should be to optimally meet children's learning needs. That carries the implicit recognition that every child's brain is unique. And whereas most brains follow a normal developmental trajectory, each is also idiosyncratic in its strengths and weaknesses for learning particular types of information.
>
> —*John Geake*

This chapter will address some common strategies for modifying tasks and concepts for students who are working below the basic expectations or struggling with learning differences. Included are proven differentiated strategies that should be used at RTI Tier 1 every day. Teachers must also add to their bags of tricks a variety of ways to provide lateral enrichment opportunities for students as they meet the standards and expectations. To provide all students with a level of challenge appropriate for their abilities, teachers must learn how to raise the bar and extend the learning beyond the grade-level standards.

Tiered Lessons

At the heart of the differentiation movement is the concept of tiered lessons. In its simplest application, tiered lesson planning allows the teacher to structure learning at multiple levels and assign different tasks within the same lesson. All students are expected to learn the same concepts or skills but may approach the learning through different methods, activities, and materials. Tiered lessons often include varying learning styles and interests, but for this description, the levels are designed around students' readiness and their abilities to understand a particular level of content. A tiered lesson focuses on a targeted standard, information, or skill but offers multiple opportunities for students to master the concepts or skills at different levels of readiness.

Tiered by Readiness and Abilities

To tier lessons, teachers must have a good understanding of the students' ability levels specific to the concepts and content to be taught. Levels of readiness are determined through preassessments and student observations (see chapter 6). This is necessary, given that we know all learners have had different environments and experiences, and thus their brains are wired differently.

The goal is for all students to achieve mastery and meet, and possibly exceed, the standard. The number of tiers created will depend on the range of learners within a class. Two or three levels are most often implemented. Tier two is the basic level of mastery all students are expected to achieve. Tier-one lessons are designed for struggling learners. Tier-three lessons are created to expand and extend learning for capable students. (See fig. 5.1.)

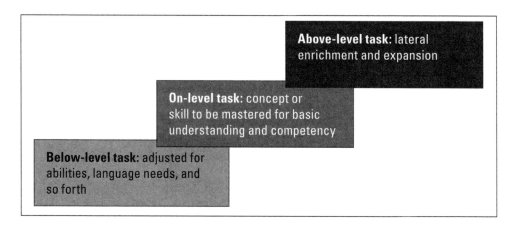

Figure 5.1: Tiered lessons.

All tiers should have interesting, engaging, and respectful tasks so that each student is appropriately engaged and challenged. The levels of tiering should challenge students just beyond their skill level to keep them in flow. The worst practice related to tiering is giving dull, boring activities to the group that is just beginning, more interesting applications to those at grade level, and engaging, challenging work to the advanced level. Table 5.1 provides language that may be used to label the three tiers.

Table 5.1: Labels for Tiered Levels

Tier One	Tier Two	Tier Three
below grade level	at grade level	above grade level
just beginning	coming along	getting good
struggling learners	capable learners	advanced learners
below basic	basic	above basic

Often a fourth tier is included for English learners (ELs). This implies that their readiness level is determined not by their cognitive abilities but by their lack of language development. Tasks would be designed with additional help or accommodations for the EL.

Students in Tier One

Students assessed to be in tier one (below basic) typically have difficulties with any one or combination of the following:

- Oral expression
- Listening comprehension
- Written expression and/or spelling
- Basic reading skills
- Mathematical calculation and/or reasoning
- Staying on task for extended periods of time—is easily distracted, poor sense of time
- Perseverance—lacks tolerance and is easily frustrated
- Following complicated directions
- Controlling emotions and/or verbal outbursts

Students assessed to be in tier one may not have a learning disability (formally identified or not); they may simply be lacking the requisite skills needed for the task (lack of experience or opportunity in the past). They may not have prior experiences with the concept and need a little time or a jump-start to catch up with the students in tier two. Students with hearing, visual, or physical impairments may need actual modifications of the task in order to achieve success, and some students may be lacking the language development to be able to complete the task at the basic level without some additional accommodations.

Students in Tier Two

Students assessed to be in tier two (basic):

- Are working at grade level in this area
- Have some prior experience(s) with the content or process
- Have some experience with the requisite skills necessary to complete the task
- Have the social skills necessary for any group or partner work
- Can work independently if required or, with some additional help and guidance, can continue to persevere
- With scaffolded instruction, will probably meet the standard and master the concept

Students in tier two, identified as being in the middle, are for the most part working at the expected grade level and have demonstrated basic readiness for the task or assignment. Teachers hope that the planned lesson will be developmentally appropriate for most of the students.

Students in Tier Three

Students assessed to be in tier three (above basic):

◆ Have demonstrated mastery or near mastery of the standard

◆ Have prior experiences with the topics or skills

◆ Have a high level of curiosity and show interest and excitement about new concepts

◆ Can work independently or with partners and groups

◆ Can follow directions and attempt to solve problems as they arise

◆ Have above-basic levels of reading, writing, and/or math skills for the grade level

Students identified as tier three learners will need additional tasks or challenges that will expand the basic lesson. The original lesson may be compacted so that they do not have to complete everything. The time gained from doing the modified assignment can be applied to an extension of the lesson that emphasizes lateral enrichment and adds depth and complexity. As figure 5.2 shows, tier-three-level learners may not necessarily accelerate upward to more challenging tasks; they may, in fact, explore the topic sideways, through lateral enrichment.

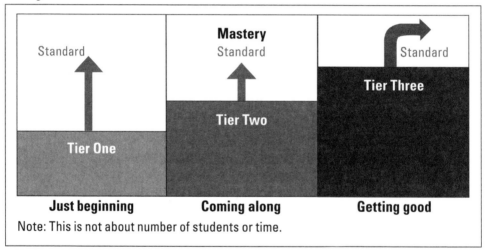

Figure 5.2: Tiered lesson steps.

Leveled lessons should only be one aspect of daily differentiation. Each task should be evaluated and students regrouped as necessary—the tiers are dynamic and change as students master concepts and catch up. They are not meant to permanently place students in ability groups. By gathering data about students and planning ahead, teachers can better address students' readiness levels with appropriate, achievable tasks that are matched to each student's zone of proximal development (Vygotsky, 1978) and help them be successful.

Tables 5.2, 5.3, and 5.4 provide examples of tiered lessons.

Table 5.2: Letter Writing, Grade 3

Tier One (Below Basic)	Tier Two (Grade Level)	Tier Three (Above Level)
Write a short, informal letter to a friend using a computer program set up with prompts. Include a heading, greeting, body (message), closing, and signature. (Use the computer model at www.abcya.com/friendly_letter_maker.htm.)	Write a friendly letter to someone (without prompts). Tell about something you have been studying. Include a heading, salutation, body, closing, and signature. You may use a computer or the fancy paper and calligraphy pens.	Write a friendly letter to someone and provide detailed information about something you are interested in. Decide on three aspects and write a paragraph on each one. Include all parts of a friendly letter. Use a computer or paper and pen.

Table 5.3: Ecosystems, Grade 7

Tier One (Below Basic)	Tier Two (Grade Level)	Tier Three (Above Level)
Use a graphic organizer (provided by the teacher) to list the producers, consumers, and decomposers for one of the ecosystems we have been studying. Find two pictures or clip art for each of the organism categories.	Select two of the ecosystems we have been studying. Create a graphic organizer to compare the organisms found in each one. Highlight the one that appears to have the widest variation of living organisms. In a paragraph, state why you think it may be endangered.	Select an ecosystem from the list provided that we have not been investigating. Design a poster that labels and illustrates the five elements of that ecosystem: soil, water, atmosphere, heat and sun, and living organisms. Provide a map of where in our region this ecosystem might be found.

Table 5.4: Classic Literature Selection, Secondary

Tier One (Below Basic)	Tier Two (Grade Level)	Tier Three (Above Level)	Tier Four (EL)
Read modified or regular text while listening to an audio recording. Read sections aloud in a guided reading circle. Watch selections from a video for clarification.	Read *Romeo & Juliet: Plainspoken* or a similar resource that provides a split text. (On one side is modern or paraphrased language, and on the facing page there is the original Shakespearean language.)	Read the actual selection. Investigate the author, setting, characters, and so forth. Investigate the theme. Compare with another selection.	Use illustrated comics, audio recordings, or video selections for support.

When creating tiered lessons, consider adjusting:

- ◆ Complexity/challenge level
- ◆ Amount of structure
- ◆ Variety of products
- ◆ Resource materials/technology
- ◆ Level of dependence
- ◆ Time allotment/pacing

Adaptations, Accommodations, and Modifications

Teachers can make adaptations to the activity or lesson when the materials are judged to be basically appropriate but need some simple adjustments to make them more manageable. Existing general education curriculum materials might be physically altered to make them more sensitive to learning needs. Providing supplemental study guides, summaries, graphic organizers, and technology support may assist some students, while others are able to read the text and complete the task without any adaptations. Teachers might adjust the pace of a lesson or the amount of material to be presented and how it is presented.

In other scenarios, teachers may need to make some accommodations (often to deal with a learning challenge such as ADHD) where they change the delivery mode or some aspects of the lesson or materials that will allow the student to successfully accomplish a task more efficiently. Providing alternative seating, presentation and response variations, accessibility, and time accommodations may help a student be successful and able to complete a task despite known learning challenges. Accommodations may need special approval (such as for assessment and testing) and may be required by law.

A *modification* usually refers to specific changes in the outcomes or standards. Modifications are made for students who, because of their intellectual, physical, or behavior disabilities, are unable to master the standard without a change or decrease in the expected outcome. Modifications fundamentally change the standard and would only be implemented when there is an individualized learning plan.

Table 5.5 may help clarify the slight differences in the terminology of these variations of differentiation.

Use Marzano's nine best practices for active processing as described in chapter 4 to help students have multiple rehearsals with new learning and strengthen dendritic growth. Research on cognitive processing and how our brains store and retrieve information can help teachers understand why certain strategies can enhance a student's ability to process new learning and solve problems. Helping learners make connections to prior knowledge, detect patterns, and learn ways to organize new information are research-based techniques that can expand our students' knowledge structures, the brain's interconnected memory networks (Rosenshine, 1997).

Table 5.5: Comparing Adaptations, Accommodations, and Modifications

Adaptations	Slight adjustments to the materials used, time allowed, seating, and amount of work—to help the student work more efficiently and independently	Shorter work times with frequent breaks Teacher-provided graphic organizers Allowed to work with a partner
Accommodations	Often legally required adaptations that ensure students diagnosed with learning disabilities have equal access to materials and an equal chance for successful learning	Differentiated texts (audio, Braille, readers) Alternative seating or setting Oral responses to test questions
Modifications	A change in the standard or outcome; an agreed-upon decrease in the course content to allow for a student's disabilities, based on each individual's special education plan to provide an equal chance for success	Special equipment or assistive devices or technology Work or testing completed at another location

 ## To Build Students' Knowledge Structures

Provide prior experiences with materials, strategies, content, and skills to build a network of background knowledge. These experiences will help build a scaffold of neural interconnections to which students may hook new learning.

Present new material in chunks and provide adequate processing time. Our working memory can only process five to seven bits of information at a time; any additional information may swamp it. A good rule of thumb is to use the ten-two theory. Teach for ten minutes, and provide at least two minutes of processing time or guided practice. Today's digital natives may have even less of an attention span than ten minutes as they are used to reacting to sound bites and rapid changes in technology. They are used to quick changes in sites and screens and have limited attention when curious about other things. Teach students how to break a task into smaller, more manageable chunks.

Help students identify patterns and provide procedural prompts. Create a phrase that repeats the steps necessary for a task (for example, to remember the steps in the algorithm of solving a division problem: divide, multiply, subtract, bring down). Establish question stems or prompts that students can repeat to themselves and use when processing new learning: Which event came first? What would happen if . . . ? What could be an alternate ending?

continued →

Create ways for students to get immediate feedback and corrections during guided practice. Practice makes permanent. Make sure students aren't practicing tasks incorrectly, and prevent them from developing misconceptions. There are four main sources for feedback and corrections: the teacher, other students, technology, and most important, a rubric or checklist provided by the teacher for self-assessing.

Jump-Starts

According to TheFreeDictionary.com, a *jump-start* is "the act or an instance of starting or setting in motion a stalled or sluggish system or process." It is not uncommon for some learners to occasionally become stalled. Their brains have perhaps lost interest, and the task is no longer novel or interesting. When multiple attempts have been made and there has been little progress, motivation and confidence wane. Providing students with some extra help and changing the task a little can often serve as a jump-start and will set learning in motion again.

Following are possible jump-starts to get students going:

- Create an anticipatory set that helps the learner see the connections to prior learning experiences. Recall similar tasks and assignments: "This activity is just like when we . . ."

- Provide teacher-made graphic organizers to assist students in seeing patterns and how information might be chunked: mind maps, T-charts, graphs, flow charts, time lines, and so on.

- Pair a struggling student with a willing capable student as study buddies for a particular task. Encourage discussions to ensure that immediate correct feedback is occurring. This can be a "yea or nay" game during which the helping student gives a thumbs-up or thumbs-down when asked if something is correct.

- Break the task or concept into chunks and help students address the new learning in small manageable steps:
  - Sort information into categories that have the same attribute(s).
  - Arrange information to show the relationships between the chunks.
  - Determine the importance, order, or time sequence of the chunks.

- Create a mnemonic device, pattern, or procedural prompt. Provide students with an acronym or a cue card to help remember the rule, phrase, or steps:
  - *I* before *E*, except after *C* or when sounded *A* as in *neighbor* and *weigh*.
  - FANBOYS stands for the seven coordinating conjunctions—*for, and, nor, but, or, yet,* and *so.*
  - The phrase "please excuse my dear aunt Sally" represents the order of operations for math—parentheses, exponents, multiply, divide, add, and subtract.

- - The phrase "kids prefer cheese over fried green spinach" represents the order of taxonomy in biology—kingdom, phylum, class, order, family, genus, and species.

  - Mnemonics in which the number of letters in each word corresponds to a digit are often used to remember numbers. For instance, this phrase gives pi to six decimal places (3.141592): How(3) I(1) wish(4) I(1) could(5) calculate(9) pi(2).

- Negotiate the amount of work that really needs to be completed. When doing math work, three calculations completed correctly could mean going on to the next level. Try giving kids free passes to use when they get stuck and want or need to move on to something else for a while.

- Provide access to a checklist or rubric so that students can get immediate feedback at each step of the learning process. Checklists provide a way to manage time and tasks, and produce a sense of accomplishment as one nears completion (see "check decks" in chapter 6).

- Arrange for alternative methods for active processing and to demonstrate mastery. For students who have difficulty writing a response, allow them to orally present the answer or draw an illustration of the process or result.

Many of these jump-starts will help various students catch up and begin to meet the basic standards for mastery. Some may be considered minor adaptations, and a few may be fairly bold accommodations. When conducting daily differentiation, teachers need to be willing to make temporary adjustments to help students take some big leaps, experience a learning breakthrough, and enjoy the feeling of success and accomplishment.

Organizing Student Tasks by Interest and Learning Preference

As discussed in the previous chapter, many differentiated strategies, such as tiered lessons, focus on the students' readiness levels and abilities. To capitalize on students' interests, experiences, and learning preferences, some activities might group learners with similar interests into small groups with specific tasks. Also, allowing students to choose the topic, task, or center activity builds self-esteem and empowerment and encourages students to extend their learning through their interests. The choice could be for a single day's activity or for a long-term project or investigation.

Choice Centers

In elementary classrooms, choice centers are a great way to allow students to explore the curriculum and have some control over what they get to do. To ensure that students complete tasks that are nonnegotiable, create a "must-do and may-do" system. The teacher assigns some of the centers to students (must-do), and then during the remaining time, the students are allowed to choose what tasks and activities they would like to do (may-do).

Have students place their name cards or name clips on the sign of the center they are choosing. Limit how many can be at a station at one time. Vary the centers using a range of learning preferences:

- **Investigation Station**—science experiments, microscopes, magnifying lenses, hands-on discovery play

- **Imagination Station**—dress-up, costumes, role-play, puppets

- **Creation Station**—art activities, drawing (materials rotate each week)

- **Communication Station**—writing materials, calligraphy, computers, iPads, cell phones

- **Calculation Station**—numbers; counting, weighing, and measuring instruments; calculators

- **Construction Station**—building materials such as wood, clay, pipe cleaners

Four Corners

Each of the four corners in the classroom is labeled. (Keep signs posted permanently to be able to use this strategy frequently.) Four colors, compass points, 1-2-3-4, and A-B-C-D can all work. Have students go to the corner that they agree with or best suits their responses. This is often called a "vote with your feet" or "vote with your body" strategy. Following are a few suggestions for using four corners:

- Use the four corners for students to express opinions: "Should kids be allowed to have TVs in their bedrooms?" (1) strongly agree, (2) agree, (3) disagree, (4) strongly disagree.

- Use the four corners for students to demonstrate their preferences: "What is your favorite fruit?" (A) apple, (B) banana, (C) orange, (D) grapes.

- Use the four corners as a way for students to show what area of study they are interested in researching: (Red) circulatory, (Blue) respiratory, (Green) digestive, (Yellow) sensory.

Jigsaw

This strategy includes the use of expert groups as part of the process. First introduced by Elliot Aronson (1978), jigsaw is an interesting and engaging as well as efficient technique for examining a large amount of content. This strategy is much more involved than those previously outlined and should not be attempted until students have developed adequate social skills to cope with larger groups and complex tasks.

Begin in base or home groups of three or four, and then follow these steps:

1. Initially, students are organized into groups of three or four members, often referred to as the base group. Each group member is given a letter or number (for example, 1, 2, 3, 4, or A, B, C, D). The material to be examined is divided into the same number of pieces as there are members in each group (three or four)

and then distributed to each member of the group. The students can be divided based on learning preferences (visual, auditory, tactile/kinesthetic) to satisfy more learners' needs. (See first line in fig. 5.3.)

2. Students form expert groups in which all the ones meet together, all the twos, and so on (see second formation in fig. 5.3). In the expert groups, the members examine the material, information, or model; analyze the critical points (the what); and decide how to share that information with their base group (the how).

3. After the experts have finished their dialogue and/or task and have reached a level of understanding, they return to their base groups (third line of fig. 5.3). Then each group member, in turn, teaches teammates what he or she has learned.

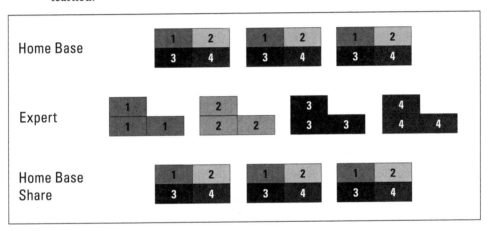

Figure 5.3: Jigsaw.

This strategy fosters interdependence as each person has a unique piece of the whole that is valuable for a shared understanding. If students are expected to understand new information thoroughly enough to share it with others, they need to carefully examine materials and use critical-thinking skills. Articulating, explaining, or interpreting new information helps students create long-term and enduring understanding.

Following is an example of jigsaw in action. Students are studying a new topic, the countries of Africa. They are assigned the areas of geography, people, wildlife, and food and agriculture. The expert groups meet and explore one of these four areas, and then the students return to their home or base groups and teach each other.

Jigsaw can be used in any subject discipline with almost any content. It can serve as an advance organizer, as a strategy for presenting information, or as a closure activity to consolidate student learning. We are incorporating three very powerful strategies in using jigsaw:

1. Cooperative group learning (social needs)

2. Using graphic organizers (visual)

3. Note taking and summarizing (critical thinking)

Lateral Enrichment and Expansion

Tier-three learners will need some additional tasks and activities to extend their learning beyond the basic level. Again, the key is preassessing all students before the lesson to discover which students have already mastered the standard or who have previous experiences and will probably get the concepts more quickly. Many times when teachers plan work for gifted learners and highly capable students, it tends to be the next-more-difficult task—using terminology in gifted education, the curriculum is "accelerated." If students complete a task and demonstrate mastery, teachers have them go on to the next assignment. Frequent acceleration of a student's school and learning experience can lead to a couple of problems in the future:

◆ The chasm between what the gifted students are learning and what the other students are learning becomes greater. The teacher has a wider range of capabilities within a class.

◆ Gifted students may become burned out as they realize that the more they show what they know, the more work and more difficult tasks they are assigned—and eventually, they could possibly be separated from friends. Students may become low-achieving gifted students.

To keep learning engaging for capable students, create opportunities to think sideways and approach a routine task with greater depth and complexity—that is, lateral enrichment. A continual balance of acceleration and extensions (see fig. 5.4) may keep students engaged and learning more challenging ways to think about things.

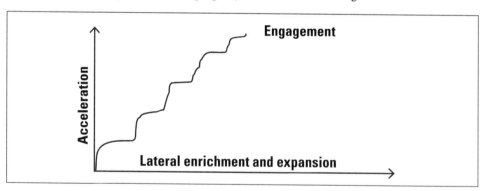

Figure 5.4: Engagement = balancing acceleration with enrichment and expansion.

Thinking Sideways, Elementary Example (Electric Circuits)

To demonstrate mastery: Create a simple electric circuit using a lightbulb, batteries, and wire.

Those who can demonstrate mastery: Integrate an "on-off" switch into the simple circuit, or create an electronic game board. Put questions in a column on the left. Put multiple-choice answers on the right. Use paper clips as conductors. Make the light go on (circuit is completed) if the user selects the correct response.

Thinking Sideways, Secondary Example (Supply and Demand)

To demonstrate mastery: Research the top five items needed by a family traveling west on the Oregon Trail in the mid 1800s. Report on the estimated costs and weights of these commodities as they began their trip in Missouri. Determine if the travelers were often paying inflated pricing.

Those who can demonstrate mastery: Research the availability of additional supplies along the Oregon Trail. Report on some of the costs of restocking the basics. Find an example of an entrepreneur who took advantage of the supply-and-demand market of the westward travelers.

 Creating Extension Tasks

To create dynamic extension tasks and inquiries, use the following formula for designing activities that go beyond routine assignments:

Process verb from a higher-order thinking strategy
(Bloom's or Williams')

+

Content perspective—depth and complexity
(Kaplan's depth and complexity icons, one or more)

+

Product possibility
(communication, representation, performance, multimedia)

=

High-quality extension task

Higher-Order Thinking Skills

As described in chapter 3, a student's level of interest may increase if the task involves working with higher-order thinking skills (HOTS) and aspects of creative thinking. Bloom's revised taxonomy emphasizes that the highest levels—analysis, evaluation, and synthesis—will involve more detailed thinking. We can use these levels when brainstorming activities that will extend learning. Use a list of process verbs for each level to help generate tasks (see table 5.6, page 104). Basic creative thinking skills are characterized by fluency, flexibility, originality, and elaboration.

Another model of higher-order thinking skills was developed by Frank E. Williams (1993) and included in his Cognitive-Affective Interaction Model for Enriching Gifted Programs. The teaching strategies shown in table 5.7 (page 104) are designed to give students opportunities for creative thinking, imagination, risk taking, and complex thinking.

Table 5.6: Process Verbs for Thinking Skills From Bloom's Taxonomy

Remembering	Understanding	Applying	Analyzing	Evaluating	Creating
remember	describe	demon-strate	compare	judge	construct
list	discuss	illustrate	analyze	evaluate	create
define	explain	dramatize	classify	select	invent
tell	summarize	apply	contrast	defend	design
label	locate	solve	experiment	support	synthesize
state	calculate	operate	question	advocate	develop

Table 5.7: Williams' Higher-Order Thinking Strategies: Six of Eighteen

Higher-Order Thinking Strategy	Example
Paradoxes	Explore self-contradictory statements or observations. "Which came first, the chicken or the egg?"
Attributes	Analyze the properties, symbols, or quantities of something.
Analogies	Find similarities between things, and make comparisons based on those similarities.
Discrepancies	Discover what is not known, and find missing links in information.
Provocative questions	Make inquiries that require thoughtful consideration.
Intuitive expression	Consider hunches and one's inward feeling about something. "What does your gut say?"

Source: Adapted from Williams, 1993.

Depth and Complexity Thinking Tools

Often, general education classroom teachers have difficulty developing challenging extension tasks to meet the needs of gifted students. *The Flip Book* by Sandra Kaplan, Bette Gould, and Victoria Siegel (1995) offers a solid description of what it means to create and build depth and complexity within a lesson. Depth means to dig deeper, extend the study, venture further, go from concrete to abstract, and elaborate. Complexity means to gain a greater breadth of understanding. Each of the categories can be used as a single thinking tool. Combine the two together and the task becomes more rigorous.

To create depth, there are eight areas of consideration: details, patterns, trends, unanswered questions, rules, ethics, big ideas, and the language of the discipline. An additional three areas are recommended to build complexity: across the disciplines, changes over time, and multiple perspectives. Each of the eleven areas has a simple representational icon to create an easy visual reference (see table 5.8). Many teachers introduce the icons to students and use them to code tasks for further study. Also known as "iconic prompts," the depth and complexity icons are used to prompt students to extend their investigations, to dig deeper, and to gain a wider perspective on their topics. (For many more suggestions regarding the use of the depth and complexity icons, visit JTaylor Education at www.jtayloreducation.com.)

Table 5.8: Depth and Complexity Icons

Area of Focus	Task to Investigate	Traits
Details	What are the attributes and defining features that characterize this?	Elements Factors Facts Specifics Traits
Patterns	What events keep occurring? What elements are expected over time? Can we predict what will happen next?	Cyclical Repetitive Systematic Sequential
Trends	What ongoing factors have influenced this event (social, economic, political)? Are there patterns of change over time?	Directions Influences Courses of action Tendencies

continued →

Area of Focus	Task to Investigate	Traits
Unanswered Questions	What is still not understood about this topic? What is yet unknown?	Unproven Unclear Unsolved Doubtful
Rules	How is this structured? What are the stated or unstated causes related to the explanation?	Structures Reasons Order Protocols
Ethics	What dilemmas or controversies are involved? Do any elements reflect bias, prejudice, or discrimination?	Conflicts Dilemmas Positions Values and morals Right and wrong
Big Idea	What overarching statement best describes this? Is there a general rule that summarizes the information?	Theme Theory Thesis Principle Generalization
Language of the Discipline	What terms or words are specific to the discipline? What tools are used? Is there a specialized vocabulary?	Terminology Phrasing Jargon Lingo Abbreviations
Across Disciplines	How do experts in one discipline learn from experts in other disciplines?	Integrate Connect Link Associate
Changes Over Time	How are these ideas related to a particular time period? Is there a relationship between past, present, and future?	Past and present Note changes over time Consider the future

Area of Focus	Task to Investigate	Traits
Multiple Perspectives	What are the opposing viewpoints? How do different people see this situation?	Points of view Roles Experts Careers

Source: Kaplan, Gould, & Siegel, 1995. Definitions of dimensions of depth and complexity are from Differentiating the Core Curriculum and Instruction to Provide Advanced Learning Opportunities, *California Department of Education and California Association for the Gifted, 1994. Symbols for dimensions of depth and complexity developed under the auspices of OERI, Javits Curriculum Project T.W.O., 1996. Used with permission.*

When designing extension tasks, be sure to include a wide range of products and performances (see table 5.9). Provide opportunities for students to express their opinions and demonstrate their new learning using a variety of engaging activities, and allow students to use technology resources and multimedia tools to show what they know.

Table 5.9: Product Possibilities for Extension Activities

Communications	Representations	Performances	Multimedia
mini-books	illustrations	role-play/skits	web design
newspapers	models	mock trial/debate	PowerPoint
brochures	blueprints	simulations	wikis/blogs
posters	inventions	volunteering	music
letters	experiments	fairs/festivals	video

Verb + Content + Product = Extension Task

When planning an extension task, use the process verbs from Bloom's taxonomy (table 5.6, page 104) and select an area of focus (content) from Williams' list (table 5.7, page 104) or the depth and complexity model (table 5.8, page 105). Then select what type of product or performance (table 5.9) might make this a great extension task.

In the following examples, look for the *verb*, the *content*, and the *product*:

♦   Research the patterns of immigration to North America in the last one hundred years using a web search. Summarize how immigration trends have changed over this time period in a brief essay. Illustrate and label on a map three regions that have received the greatest number of new immigrants in the last thirty years. Use Google Earth online if available.

- Analyze at least twenty pea pods and tally how many peas were found in each. Calculate the average number of peas in each one. Design a bar graph using a simple chart on PowerPoint to display your results.

- Create a mini-book of the definitions for the main terms we have been using in our "floaters and sinkers" unit (*sink, float, surface tension, density, weight, volume*). Include definitions and simple illustrations. Or you may take photos with the digital camera and insert them into your booklet.

- Compare two points of view about which route to take from the school to your house. Option 1: using a GPS handheld device (or iPhone app), travel the routes to determine the actual distance and travel times. Option 2: plot the routes on Google Maps and record the estimated distances and travel times. Write a persuasive letter to your parents and tell them which route you recommend.

There are numerous resources and websites that can assist you in designing quality extension activities. Investigate the Byrdseed website (www.byrdseed.com/differentiator), which is dedicated to ideas for teaching gifted students. Visit ExtendAMenu (www.extendamenu.com/index.php) for assistance in building choice lists, tic-tac-toe boards, and such. A wide variety of helpful downloadable tools and products for depth and complexity are available at JTaylor Education (www.jtayloreducation.com).

Anchor Activities

When students work on different activities at different times, some finish before others. When classrooms are set up for students to rotate to different stations or centers, sometimes there are wait times as some groups progress more slowly than others. This ragged time in a classroom is a fertile place for behavioral problems to emerge. With nothing to do, students often start wandering and distracting others. Having a go-to task for all students can alleviate many of these problems.

When implementing daily differentiation, a key to success will be having a plan for what students should be doing if they are finished before others or are waiting their turns. Originally defined by Tomlinson (1999b), anchor activities are specified ongoing tasks put in place for students to do during ragged times (see fig. 5.5). Educators may "provide a list of possible anchor options and should encourage students to suggest other ideas. Anchor activities must be important to essential student learning and never just time-fillers" (Tomlinson & Strickland, 2005, p. 349).

Anchor activities should:

- Be self-directed
- Include aspects that can be completed on an ongoing basis
- Relate to the concepts and content to be learned
- Not necessarily involve other students
- Be engaging, meaningful tasks—not busywork or packets of worksheets

◆ Be activities that everyone will eventually have a chance to do, even if not yet finished with other work

This Week's Anchor Activity
Create a travel brochure about Australia. Your brochure should include:
- *At least five spelling words from this week's list*
- *A written description of the country and its people*
- *Drawings of some of Australia's animals*
- *A list of fun facts*

Figure 5.5: Anchor activity example.

To help students understand how anchor activities will work, begin with a basic task for everyone that will be done independently and silently. During the anchor activity work time, meet with individual students or small groups. Get the class used to the idea that unless you have another teacher-assigned task, you should keep working on your anchor activity. Remember that a great anchor is meaningful, engaging, and can be worked on in small increments.

Examples of beginning anchor activities include:

◆ Creating a brochure about the topic

◆ Preparing and practicing for an oral presentation

◆ Writing letters to get more information about the topic

◆ Collecting pictures about the topic online or from magazines for a bulletin board

◆ Finding amazing facts online or in resource books and posting them

◆ Working on a rough draft of a current writing assignment

◆ Finishing up a checklist of miscellaneous work

As the class becomes used to having various activities going on at the same time, the complexity of the anchor activity can be developed based on the developmental capabilities of the students. Anchors can be tiered with several levels of depth and difficulty. Some preplanning will help teachers create great anchors that are powerful learning activities as well as helpful differentiated strategies:

◆ What indicators, outcomes, standards, or concepts will be emphasized?

◆ What will the students be expected to complete independently?

◆ Will the activity be part of a group project?

◆ How is the activity differentiated or tiered to address various ability levels?

◆ What instruction must be given so that all students understand how to do the task?

- Are there aspects of the project that can be worked on at irregular (ragged) times?

- What materials will be needed for completing the activity and for independent work?

- May any part of the task be worked on at home?

Because anchors are not busywork, they must be thought through carefully. Consider how much class time will be allotted so that all students will have some time to complete the basic assignment. Those students who are often done early will accrue more time to work on the task, and there should be a higher level of expectation when they've completed the activity. Take time to reflect on the following questions to effectively orchestrate the anchor activity:

- When will all students have time to work on the task(s)?

- What other opportunities will students have to work?

- At what point must the activity be totally completed?

- What kind of benchmarks or checkpoints might be implemented?

- What method of ongoing assessment will be available to the students to get feedback along the way?

- What will the activity be worth as a grade?

- What will the criteria be for the final evaluation? A rubric?

- Would a contract or checklist be helpful to encourage independence?

- What are the procedures if students need help, are finished, or are waiting?

Ongoing Anchors

Ongoing anchors are often centers or stations that students can go to whenever they are done. Some classrooms have the standing rule that if you are finished you may do DEAR (Drop Everything and Read) or complete work that needs to be finished. Or there may be a particular study kit or program or a computer task that may be worked on when students are finished with other work.

Everybody's Doin' It

Some anchor activities have the same basic assignment for all. Each student is to complete the task, and it is a requirement that must be done. It may be tiered so that the different levels of learners within the classroom have different completion requirements. It could be a poster or brochure that everyone is assigned.

Must-Do . . . May-Do

In some classrooms, when students finish the required nonnegotiable assignments, they get to choose an anchor activity. Several types of activities are offered, representing different learning preferences and products. Limit choices at first to reduce stress and anxiety.

Group Projects

Small groups of students can be assigned a project, model, presentation, or other larger task. Jobs and responsibilities should be divided and shared fairly (not always equally) based on each student's strengths and talents. Each member of the group should have aspects of the project that can be completed independently. If a student happens to be finished and has time to work on the project, he or she shouldn't have to wait for the rest of the group in order to begin working. Group checklists are helpful. The grading procedure(s) should be introduced at the beginning of the assignment.

Learning Celebration

A terrific way to end an interesting unit is for the whole class to plan a culminating activity and invite an audience of family, students, or the community. This celebration of learning might be a fair, a festival, a presentation, an authors' night, or a museum that showcases the students' work. Each student might have an assignment that he or she is personally responsible for as well as inclusion in a group project. The anchor activity and the culminating project are one and the same.

Simulations

A whole-class simulation is an exciting way to create ongoing student tasks during the course of a unit. Mock trials, elections, or debates help students role-play and prepare for a culminating event. Interact Simulations (www.interact-simulations.com) has a vast assortment of detailed simulations with a social studies and history focus. While these simulations can take up a lot of time, the students can really learn a lot.

Simulations are often completed online. If the technology is available, students can participate in virtual projects and complete them over time online. A terrific source for simulation activities in math and science (grades 3–12) is ExploreLearning (www.explore learning.com), which claims to have the largest library of interactive online learning simulations called "Gizmos."

WebQuests

Another web-based project that makes a terrific anchor activity is a WebQuest. A WebQuest is an inquiry project students complete online about a particular topic or event. Bernie Dodge, at San Diego State University, developed the original model in 1995. Now, WebQuests can be created by a teacher in Word, PowerPoint, and even Excel or produced by a commercial designer. WebQuests have a few critical attributes. WebQuest.org (2007) states that a real WebQuest:

- Is wrapped around a doable and interesting task that is ideally a scaled down version of things that adults do as citizens or workers.
- Requires higher level thinking, not simply summarizing. This includes synthesis, analysis, problem-solving, creativity and judgment.
- Makes good use of the web. A WebQuest that isn't based on real resources from the web is probably just a traditional lesson in disguise. (Of course, books and other media can be used within a WebQuest, but if the web isn't at the heart of the lesson, it's not a WebQuest.)
- Isn't a research report or a step-by-step science or math procedure. Having learners simply distilling web sites and making a presentation about them isn't enough.
- Isn't just a series of web-based experiences. Having learners go look at this page, then go play this game, then go here and turn your name into hieroglyphs doesn't require higher level thinking skills and so, by definition, isn't a WebQuest.

A great resource for WebQuest templates is an educational technology group from the University of Regina (www.educationaltechnology.ca/resources). Quest Garden (http://questgarden.com) is another resource (subscription based) on creating and sharing WebQuest ideas.

A compelling analogy likens the art of differentiating instruction to fishing. As teachers, we prepare our lessons with our best lures, hoping to catch most of the learners. When the students simply aren't going for the strategy, educators need to be prepared to change the bait. When we speak about extending learning, we mean in all directions! Sometimes we need to get rid of barriers and adjust assignments for struggling learners. Consider raising the bar for many students by creating extension possibilities that increase the learning with lateral enrichment.

Chapter Review

Designing Tiered Lessons: The one-size-fits-all approach to curricular design may meet the students in the middle but fail to address the needs of struggling students, ELs, and students with special needs. Tiered lesson planning allows the teacher to structure learning at multiple levels and assign different tasks within the same lesson. All students are expected to learn the same concepts or skills but may approach them through different methods, activities, and materials.

- Tiered by readiness, *page 92*
- Sample tiered lessons, *page 95*
- Adaptations, accommodations, and modifications, *page 96*
- Jump-starts, *page 98*

Organizing Tasks by Student Interests and Preferences: To capitalize on students' interests and learning preferences, some activities might group the learners into small groups with specific tasks. Allowing students to choose the topic, task, or center activity builds self-esteem and empowerment.

- Choice centers, *page 99*
- Four corners, *page 100*
- Jigsaw, *page 100*

Adding Depth and Complexity: To keep learning engaging for capable students, create opportunities to think sideways and approach a routine task with greater depth and complexity.

- Lateral enrichment, *page 102*
- Higher-order thinking skills (HOTS), *page 103*
- Depth and complexity icon tools, *page 105*
- Anchor activities for ragged times, *page 108*
- WebQuests, *page 111*

6

Evaluating the Learning

Frequent formative assessment and corrective feedback are powerful tools to promote long-term memory and develop the executive functions of reasoning and analysis. Frequent assessment provides teachers information about students' minute-to-minute understanding during instruction.

—Judy Willis

In this high-stakes environment, teachers are striving heroically to help all students be successful. There is a huge push to increase student success and show well in international comparisons such as the Trends in International Mathematics and Science Study (TIMSS) tests. Differentiation is necessary for success because of the differences in the brains of our learners:

- Their prior knowledge and experience

- Their interests and preferences

- Their rate of grasping new concepts and understandings

- The number of rehearsals that are needed to reach mastery

We recognize the need to differentiate instruction, but what does this mean for assessment practices? If students are different and have different needs, then we must also give them multiple ways of demonstrating understanding or mastery over time without penalty for rate of learning. To accurately evaluate student learning, assessments should focus on authentic achievements, genuine products, and creative performances. Assessments must be aligned with how brains learn best.

Educators who have focused on standards and assessments report that the role of the teacher is to ensure success for all learners (Wiggins, 1998; Stiggins, 2001; Earl, 2003; Reeves, 2008). Assessment guides instruction and informs both the teacher and the student of where they are in the teaching/learning process. In this chapter, we will explore the essence of assessment, including the language and terminology of assessment and its impact on learning.

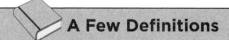

A Few Definitions

Clarity of terms is important when educators are discussing teaching and learning issues. Various forms of assessment can be used continually to inform daily instruction.

Assessment comes from Latin; *assess* means "to sit beside." Tax assessors sat beside citizens to assess their taxes. The assessment of students and their work is a "sitting beside" process that involves a variety of methods.

Preassessment: assessment that is applied before the unit of study begins to provide data for the planning process. There are many quick techniques that can be used as preassessments to obtain information about readiness, prior knowledge and experience, interests, and learning profiles.

Formative assessment: an ongoing check for understanding that is necessary to make sure students are making progress toward the standard. This type of assessment occurs while the learning is taking place. It provides information that informs the next steps and leads to improvement in the process. Formative assessment also includes the student in the process.

Summative assessment: assessment after the learning time is completed, used to assign a final grade. The summative assessment or evaluation is the demonstration of the level of mastery that students have acquired. Teachers then assign a grade by placing a value on the learning related to the competency or expectation.

Guidelines for Assessment

The following are guidelines for teachers when thinking about assessment:

- Teachers should be clear about the outcomes/standards/expectations that are being targeted in the lesson or unit of study. It's important to know the destination before you start the journey.

- These same outcomes/standards/expectations should be shared with the learners. Students have a far better chance of being successful if it is clear where they are headed.

- Assessments measure the targeted standards. This seems unnecessary to say, yet many assignments provide a grade for the gradebook but not information about growth toward the standard.

- Feedback is specific, timely, and helpful to the student to increase continual growth. The brain relies on feedback to strengthen connections and sometimes correct an understanding or concept. Specific feedback tells the brain what to store and what to discard. Feedback provides the next steps in the clarification and/or skill development process.

- Assessments should inform everyone's efforts, both students' and teachers'.

- Data from formative assessments is used to improve instruction.
- In a differentiated classroom, it is important to gather ongoing data that will be used to keep adjusting and redesigning the learning.

Getting to Know Your Students

If we intend to respond to the uniqueness of our students, we need to get to know them. Students reveal their personalities, interests, and preferences through the choices they make, and this data can be collected through overt surveys and inventories. If you Google or Bing "multiple intelligences tests or surveys," several websites will give you resources for use in the classroom. Some online surveys provide immediate feedback and profiling. Similarly, there are sites to assess learning styles and preferences.

Some websites that might be helpful include:

- Lumosity: www.lumosity.com
- Multiple Intelligences for Adult Literacy and Education: http://literacyworks .org/mi/home.html
- Concept to Classroom: www.thirteen.org/edonline/concept2class/mi/index .html

Surveys in specific subject areas help teachers understand their students' interests, prior knowledge, preferences, skills, concerns, self-awareness, and expectations. With this information, teachers can better attend to the preferences and needs of the students by creating learning experiences that fit their profiles. Following are examples of math survey questions:

- I am taking this course because _____.
- I enjoy _____ in math.
- I am worried about _____.
- I learn best when _____.
- One request I have is _____.

Asking students to react to the learning by using a "plus, minus, and interesting" exit card can provide feedback regarding the enjoyment of the learning experience:

- Plus (what I enjoyed)
- Minus (what didn't work well for me today)
- Interesting (an aha moment or connection of interest)

Preassessments

Preassessing provides teachers with information prior to the learning process:

- What students already know

- What misconceptions exist
- What groupings might work
- What interests students have
- What gaps exist

Preassessments can be given before every chunk of a new concept, unit, or skill is taught. After a teacher uses a preassessment tool, the data are used to plan the learning experiences. The teacher will know students' background or prior knowledge so as not to repeat content. Misconceptions can be identified. Interests or questions of interest can be built into the unit.

We know that novelty, interest, and meaning intrigue the brain, and we can use information from preassessments to capture those three key elements. The degree of detail or expertise that students bring to the new learning can also provide the ability to group the students by readiness and produce that "flow" environment where challenge just exceeds skill level so that students believe that they can succeed but also have to stretch their thinking and skill.

While it may seem like preassessing may not be worth the time spent, it actually saves time by making the planning more precise and specific. There are several quick, low-prep strategies for preassessment.

3-2-1 Exit Cards

One low-prep preassessment asks students to fill in 3-2-1 exit cards a week before the unit of study to find out:

- 3 things they know about the topic
- 2 questions they have
- 1 suggestion or request they might have

These don't have to be formal, printed cards. Just a sticky note and directions on the overhead will work.

Another variation might be:

- 3 things they would like to investigate
- 2 people they'd like to work with
- 1 question they have

You can also use 3-2-1 cards as a do-now assignment at the start of class to connect to the last class:

- 3 things they remember about . . .
- 2 connections
- 1 question they still have

K-W-L

K-W-L (Ogle, 1986) is another quick and easy preassessment to find out what prior knowledge and interests students have. K represents what students know about the topic; W represents what students want to know or wonder about; and L represents what the students have learned (see table 6.1).

Table 6.1: K-W-L

K What I know	W What I want to know or wonder about	L What I learned

An individual K-W-L is more illuminating than a class or group K-W-L and indicates what each student knows and wants to know. Just a small slip of paper folded into three columns gives each student an individual preassessment. Teachers learn what the students already know about the topic, any misconceptions they hold, and what their interests in the subject are.

T-Chart

A T-chart is just two columns that can be headed up with any criteria. Table 6.2 is an example of a T-chart.

Table 6.2: T-Chart Preassessment

What I know about _____	Questions I have

Students will get bored using the same strategy every time, so it is best to provide some variety in your preassessments.

Formative Assessments

Gone are the days when we could ask students, "Do you understand?" and rely on heads nodding to affirm comprehension. We need concrete proof that they do or do not understand. Differentiation is about everybody getting it, and if they are going to get it, it may take different ways on different days. We have to keep checking the oil to see if there is enough. In the classroom, we don't have just one dipstick. We have many ways to check for understanding. And we have to do it often throughout the class and the day.

After checking for understanding, we must decide what is needed and who needs it. We may find that some students have an in-depth understanding or skill level and need something challenging. Some students may have a general understanding and need more rehearsal, and another group may need a different approach or reteaching.

A 3-2-1 exit card can be used to inform the teacher where the student is right now in his or her learning. Four corners can be used to assess students' degrees of proficiency. Any assessment that is useful to plan for learning is a form of checking for understanding.

Feedback Is the Breakfast of Champions

Consider this all-too-familiar scenario. A student comes home from school for the weekend and announces that she received a B on her essay. She is upset and wants to do better. When her parents ask what the teacher suggested for improvement, she notes that there are no suggestions, just a B at the top. When the student inquires of the teacher on Monday, the teacher says he knows a B essay when he sees one.

People don't get better because of grading; they get better because of feedback. Students improve through the use of specific, suggestive feedback and wait time (Black, Harrison, Lee, Marshall, & Wiliam, 2004; Black & Wiliam, 2009). To become capable and competent, anyone in the process of learning new skills or content/concepts needs positive feedback related to a task well done and corrective feedback about a task still being learned. No coach grades a sports play; he or she points out the good aspects and makes suggestions for the next time in a positive, corrective, directive way. Most learners try to improve and succeed and are better able to do so with help, support, and suggestions.

All this makes sense when we consider that it is the presence of feedback that helps the brain fine-tune the dendritic connections and patterns. Without feedback, erroneous connections may be made and cause "cumulative ignorance" over time. The brain thrives on challenge and is inhibited by threat (Caine & Caine, 1997; Csikszentmihalyi, 1990) and needs safety, positive feedback, and encouragement to continue to grow. We know that the brain's main purpose is survival, and it pays attention to important information and responds with focus. A task that is novel, in the zone of proximity, and seems doable is amenable to the brain. If students believe that they can handle the situation and are receiving the coaching and the positive feedback they need, their brain releases dopamine, the pleasure neurotransmitter that also helps in the memory process (Storm & Tecott, 2005). Perseverance also comes from this dopamine release and helps students with the intrinsic motivation to continue the task (Gee, 2007). The brain responds to challenge and, if given specific feedback, will form intentions and goals and will accomplish them with attention and persistence (Haynes et al., 2007).

Effective feedback has two main aspects:

1. **The cognitive factor**. Good feedback shows students where they are in the learning and what to do next.

2. **The motivational factor.** When students understand what to do and why, most students develop a feeling that they have control over their own learning.

A Paul Black and Dylan Wiliam (2009) study showed that if there were grades and feedback on an assignment, the student paid more attention to the grade (his or her ranking) and ignored the suggestions. But without the grade, the feedback guided the student in his or her next effort. It was a "feed forward" mechanism that seemed to work. This feedback process can be very time consuming if only done by the teacher, and that directive critic process is not helping students become critical and self-reflective. Therefore, students need to become critics of quality work, peer to peer and through self-assessment using rubrics or criteria and metacognitive strategies that include logs and journals.

Marc Prensky (2010) encourages educators to use technological resources to orchestrate opportunities for immediate feedback. For example, posting writings, videos, and such on the web for real audiences to see can provide terrific responses and feedback. And when students can see the work of other students, it gives them a framework with which to measure their own success and progress. Peer editing and rubrics are also valuable tools for the feedback and improvement process.

Peer Editing

As noted previously, assessment is from the Latin, "to sit beside." The teacher is not the only one available to sit beside the student and give feedback. Other students can be helpful in critiquing the quality of work and giving feedback. They can learn to compliment strengths and make helpful suggestions. As students compare the product to a list of criteria or rubric, they deepen their own understanding of quality work, and the conversation and feedback help both students improve their product, performance, or task.

Rubrics

Rubrics are excellent resources that give students a better chance of hitting the target as the target is made clear. Well-constructed rubrics "provide a way for teachers to provide students with feedback that tells them what they are learning, how well they are progressing, and what they must do to improve. Rubrics as scoring guides explain levels of performance, often on a 1 to 4 scale, and help students focus on the learning" (Westerberg, 2009).

The process is multipurpose:

+ A rubric shows clearly what is expected in the task. It provides articulated, detailed criteria and descriptors so that students know before the undertaking what is expected and will be valued and judged. No "gotchas" here.

+ A rubric serves as a guide as students work to identify important aspects of the project or work, and students can self-check as they go along. They refine their work on an ongoing basis.

+ A rubric can also be used as a scoring guide to grade the final product based on the criteria. Different criteria can be weighted to create a grade with more weight placed on more critical elements.

◆   Students can reflect on the final product and note criteria that need improvement for next time. Portfolios and logs or journals are valuable tools for this aspect of the assessment. Setting personal goals is a lifelong skill, and being clear about what needs improvement and what has been mastered adds clarity to students' thinking and helps them to self-direct their learning.

RubiStar (http://rubistar.4teachers.org) is a great website for building rubrics.

Table 6.3 is a rubric for a group investigation.

In your quest to design quality rubrics, consider the following:

◆   Does the rubric assess what you want assessed?

◆   Is the rubric clear and understandable for the students?

◆   How will the student's self-assessment (using the rubric) help you plan?

Keep in mind that students will better internalize the important criteria if they play a part in the process of building the rubric for their project or task.

An Adjustable Moment

Teachers plan lessons and units and proceed as planned, yet conditions vary based on how easily or with what difficulty students deal with the new information or skill. Teachers should integrate an opportunity to gather data on student progress and mastery within the lessons. We call this creating an "adjustment opportunity." (See fig. 6.1, page 124.)

With feedback collected, the teacher may decide to reteach the whole group, divide the group, or move the whole group on. The process varies; following is one scenario:

1.   Preassess or gather data prior to the lesson. A ticket out might be used with a 3-2-1 a few days before the lesson, providing a sense of where students are.

2.   Conduct whole-group instruction—a clever, engaging direct instruction with all students.

3.   Ask all students to participate in a task to start building their understanding; this could be done as individuals, partners, or small groups.

4.   Determine who is ready for the next step and who needs more time.

Students may self-assess their own understanding: "If you are stuck on something, meet me at the back table for a quick jump-start, and then I have a task to help you get better." Or perhaps, "If you are done and this task was fairly easy for you, you are ready for an extension activity." There may be a rubric to determine if the student has mastered or completed the task. If so, he or she may go on to the extension activity. If not, he or she is regrouped and has a do-over opportunity with some reteaching help.

This can be referred to as an adjustment opportunity—students are regrouped, and now there are two sets of tasks going on in the room at the same time.

Table 6.3: Group Investigation Rubric

Category	4	3	2	1
Research Questions	Independent identification of three or more insightful, reasonable, creative questions to pursue	Independent identification of three or more reasonable questions to pursue	With some adult help, identification of three or more reasonable questions to pursue	Identification, with considerable adult help, of three or more reasonable questions to pursue
Plan for Organizing Information	A clear plan for organizing the information as it is gathered and in the final research product. All students can independently explain the planned organization of the research findings.	A clear plan for organizing the information in the final research product. All students can independently explain this plan.	A clear plan for organizing the information as it is gathered. All students can independently explain most of this plan.	No clear plan for organizing the information, and/or students in the group cannot explain their organizational plan.
Quality of Sources	Independently locates at least two reliable, interesting information sources for each question	Independently locates at least two reliable information sources for each question	With some adult help, locates at least two reliable information sources for each question	With much adult help, locates at least two reliable information sources for each question
Delegation of Responsibility	Each student in the group can clearly explain what information is needed by the group, what information he or she is responsible for locating, and when the information is needed.	Each student in the group can clearly explain what information he or she is responsible for locating.	Each student in the group can, with minimal prompting from peers, clearly explain what information he or she is responsible for locating.	One or more students in the group cannot clearly explain what information they are responsible for locating.
Group Time Line	Independently develops a reasonable, complete time line describing when different parts of the work (such as planning, research, first draft, final draft) will be done. All students in the group can independently describe the main points of the time line.	Independently develops a time line describing when most parts of the work will be done. All students in the group can independently describe the main points of the time line.	Independently develops a time line describing when most parts of the work will be done. Most students can independently describe the main points of the time line.	Group needs adult help to develop a time line, and/or several students in the group cannot independently describe the main points of the time line.

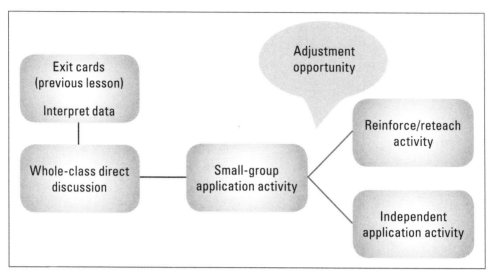

Figure 6.1: Adjustment opportunity in a lesson sequence.

The Power of Do-Overs

In a brain-friendly differentiated classroom, opportunities to redo a task and to have a second chance for success should be frequent and an integral part of the learning process. If the student has completed a task incorrectly and doesn't have a chance to do it over in a timely fashion, we run the risk of allowing his or her brain to store the wrong method or answer. A do-over allows the brain to reprogram and make sure that the correction has been made. Sometimes students object to redoing a task. They see it as boring or repetitive and don't recognize its worth in the learning process. It is important to help them understand three things that do-overs offer:

1. They enhance memory.

2. They help create memory through developing mental schemata or patterns that the brain prefers.

3. They prompt improvements and refine learning.

In order to survive, all organisms must do two things:

> They have to gather information about their environment and themselves (*perception*) and based on this information, they have to manipulate their environment, and themselves, in a way that is advantageous to them (*action*). As a result of acting, the organism gets feedback—new information from the world and from itself. That feedback provides the guidance about how the organism needs to act next time. (Fuster, 2003, as cited in Caine & Caine, 2007)

Simply put, this is the learning process. Learning is dependent upon experience. So, if students don't reach mastery with one experience, they need another. Time is, as always, of the essence, so we want to provide meaningful ways to process or explore new content and skills. When they have the opportunity to practice more than once and reflect, they can:

- Check out multiple results
- Note similarities
- Discover patterns
- Look for ahas or discrepant events
- Test hypotheses and make modifications
- Create programs, templates, and schemata for future references

Students and teachers can learn to use assessment as a gauge of learning and to make adjustments in rehearsal toward mastery by using the feedback generated from the teacher, from peers, and through self-reflection. Not only will this assessment help create precision and specificity in the learning experience, it will help students to be lifelong learners by using metacognitive processes and reflection.

Summative Assessments

At the end of the learning experience, teachers need to provide a final assessment to garner information related to the total learning experience. Some summative assessments are more suited to content outcomes and some to processes or skills (see table 6.4).

In a differentiated classroom, choice is an important component, but along with choice, there needs to be a clear target and students need criteria to guide them in the preparation of the culminating performance, exhibition, or project. When teachers offer choice opportunities for student-created products and performances, they will be amazed at the creativity students will demonstrate.

Crystal-clear criteria for each task will help students self-assess their work prior to turning it in for a grade or final evaluation. Create a deck of checklists for a variety of the frequently used tasks, a check deck, to answer the many questions that students might ask as they begin a task. Though check decks require some preparation initially, they can be used multiple times and encourage student independence and responsibility.

Table 6.4: Types of Outcomes

Content Outcomes	Process Outcomes
Projects and Products	**Checklists**
dioramas	individual, peer
models	group
projects	teacher
maps	
research	
video productions	
portfolios	

continued →

Content Outcomes	Process Outcomes
Pencil-and-Paper Tests matching multiple choice fill in the blanks essay	**Observations** video group members teacher
Performances speeches presentations demonstrations music, dance performances exhibitions	**Logs** factual information data for reaction time management logs and journals personal reflection goal setting metacognition

Determine the nonnegotiables that you expect of the summative tasks that are used routinely. Create a checklist for each and print these on index cards. They can include graphics and icons to make them easily understood. Gather the cards together into a deck. The following are variations for using check decks:

◆ Variation 1—Print and laminate the cards. Punch a hole in the corner of each card and gather the deck together on a key ring. Hang the deck on a hook for students to refer to.

◆ Variation 2—Run multiple copies of the checklists (different colors for different tasks). Put copies of each checklist in a pocket posted on a bulletin board. Students may take a copy of the checklist and attach it to the task as they are working on it.

Following are example checklists.

Create a Tri-Fold Brochure:

❑ Fold the brochure neatly.

❑ Use all panels.

❑ Decorate the front cover and clearly print the title.

❑ Check all spelling.

❑ Make sure all icons, graphics, and illustrations are neat and colorful.

❑ Include required number of accurate facts and details.

Create a Display Poster:

- ❑ Use heavy 12 × 18" tagboard.
- ❑ Make title at least 2 inches high and use neat capital letters.
- ❑ Create bullet points.
- ❑ Add colorful, neat graphics.
- ❑ Make sure it can be read easily from 6 feet away.
- ❑ Include accurate facts.

Chapter Review

Defining Assessment: Providing clarity on assessment terms

- ◆ Preassessment, *page 116*
- ◆ Formative assessment, *page 116*
- ◆ Summative assessment, *page 116*

Using Assessment: Using assessment helps teachers plan with more precision

- ◆ Getting to know your students, *page 117*
- ◆ Preassessing before learning, *page 117*
- ◆ Checking for understanding, *page 119*

Types of Assessments: Low-prep/high-yield strategies to gather information about students' prior knowledge, interests, and preferences

- ◆ Surveys, *page 117*
- ◆ 3-2-1 exit cards, *page 118*
- ◆ K-W-L, *page 119*
- ◆ T-chart, *page 119*

Feedback: Recognizing the value of feedback to student learning

- ◆ Rubrics, *page 121*
- ◆ Adjustable moments, *page 122*
- ◆ Do-overs, *page 124*
- ◆ Check decks, *page 125*

Think Big, Start Small

Think big, start small, act now.

—*Barnabas Suebu*

Good teachers take all they know about the brain, researched best practices, and student differences and creatively plan multiple opportunities for students to be successful. In addition, educators must acknowledge the differences in learners of the 21st century. With the daily use of technology, students' brains are wiring in new and unique ways. By considering some of the major differences, we may be able to understand how this generation is changing how school must be done. In his book *Grown Up Digital*, Don Tapscott (2009) summarizes eight differentiating characteristics of our students:

1. They want *freedom* in everything they do, from freedom of choice to freedom of expression.
2. They love to *customize*, personalize.
3. They are the new *scrutinizers*.
4. They look for *corporate integrity and openness* when deciding what to buy and where to work.
5. The Net Gen wants *entertainment and play* in their work, education, and social life.
6. They are the *collaboration and relationship* generation.
7. The Net Gen has a need for *speed*—and not just in video games.
8. They are the *innovators* . . . looking for innovative ways to collaborate, entertain themselves, learn, and work. (pp. 34–36)

Tapscott suggests that as we seek to educate our students, we should seek what we might learn with them and from them.

Celebrate the ways in which you already address students' various needs. Grab a handful of new strategies or some variations on some things you already are doing. Take baby steps and start small. Trying too many new ideas may frustrate you and your students. Do a few well, and then keep adding a new one here and there. We likened differentiation to an elephant, and the old joke tells us that we eat an elephant one bite at a time.

We need to help parents and students understand the concept and the rationale for differentiation—we all have different backgrounds and experiences, interests, and preferences, and learning opportunities should reflect these differences and provide multiple ways of approaching understanding and developing skills. It is not a mystical strategy or technique that will ensure success for all, but it isn't one size that supposedly fits all either. Helping people understand what differentiation is and is not (see table 7.1) is important so that everyone is comfortable and not threatened by different tasks and time lines in the classroom. Remind students that they are similar but different, and relate those differences to their strengths and areas to celebrate as well as areas to work on and continue to grow.

Table 7.1: Identifying the Attributes of Differentiation

What It Isn't	What It Is
Tracking	Flexible grouping
A new strategy	Student centered
Static	Based on readiness
Teaching to the middle	For all learners
Individualized instruction	Changing all the time
Lowering the bar	Meeting personal interests and preferences
	Recognizing academic success

Planning Guide

Table 7.2 is a planning guide for differentiated instruction. A blank planning template can be found on page 137.

Table 7.2: Planning Guide for Differentiated Instruction

Lesson Title / Goal	Standards
	What students should know and be able to do—unifying concepts and processes
Content, Skills, and Dispositions	**Strategies and Tools**
Key concepts, processes, thinking skills	Concepts that address learning goals and essential questions on which to base activities and experiences
Know the Learner	**Strategies and Tools**
Interests, readiness, preferences	Preassessments, quizzes, surveys, K-W-L, "all about me" journals
Preassess; use data to inform methods, strategies, and grouping patterns; consider a variety of approaches to learning.	Consider: multiple intelligences, learning profiles, prior knowledge, gender and cultural biases

Design a Brain-Compatible Environment	Strategies and Tools
Create a safe and secure climate, encourage mindfulness and reflection, provide a body-compatible environment, design appropriate seating and grouping, establish classroom procedures, promote relationships and community.	Furniture, flow, groups Management systems Meet basic needs
Engage, Excite, Energize!	**Strategies and Tools**
Stimulate the learner's interest in the topic, promote curiosity, inspire participation, activate prior knowledge.	Video clips, field trips, speakers, discrepant events, questioning, demonstrations, hands-on experiences
Explore	**Strategies and Tools**
Encourage investigation, provide multiple rehearsals, chunk information, discover patterns.	Problem-based and project-based learning, action research, stations/centers, choice inquiries, group activities
Extend and Expand	**Strategies and Tools**
Provide strategies for struggling learners, expand basic understandings, build depth and complexity, design lateral enrichment opportunities.	Technology integration, multimedia, action research, community/service project
Evaluate and Assess	**Strategies and Tools**
Preassess learners for readiness; orchestrate frequent, ongoing formative assessments; provide accurate feedback to students; create meaningful summative assessments.	Rubrics, teacher-made tests, products and presentations, portfolios, journals/notebooks

Table 7.3 provides a sample planning guide for an eighth-grade lesson on mindsets to get you started.

Table 7.3: Sample Planning Guide, Growing Smarter Brains (Grade 8)

Lesson Title / Goal	Standards
"Growing Smarter Brains: How EVERYONE Can Increase Their Intelligence!" (growth and fixed mindsets)	1.3.M Identify qualities that contribute to a positive self-image. 2.1.G Analyze internal and external influences that can affect growth and development, relationships . . .

continued →

Content, Skills, and Dispositions	Strategies and Tools
Multisensory experiences in an enriched environment can stimulate brain growth and development. With a growth mindset and effort, one can continue to get smarter throughout one's life. One's self-talk and feedback from others can influence his or her mindset (fixed or growth).	Review content and identify concepts that address: • Neural plasticity • Fixed and growth mindsets (Dweck, 2006) • Our internal dialogues • Traits of successful people
Know the Learner 35% are English learners. Two classes have many identified resource learners. Students are interested in pop culture, music, and sports figures.	**Strategies and Tools** PPT: "What does it mean to be smart?" Think-pair-share PPT: "Are people born smart? Who is smarter?" Multiple choice, group discussion PPT: "What areas of your brain are already dense? What areas would you like to grow?"
Design a Brain-Compatible Environment Present guest teacher—provide introduction/background. Show PPT presentation—check lighting and sound. Review procedures.	**Strategies and Tools** Students sit at table groups of four Process partners Graphic organizer for note taking provided Red/green response cards—cups for tables
Engage, Excite, Energize! Show PPT: "Are we born already good at math, sports, art, and so on?" Show PPT: "Diamond's neural plasticity experiments with rats" Show "9 dots" puzzle and optical illusion clip—keep trying!	**Strategies and Tools** Video clip: Michael Jordan Visuals: brains, neurons, rats, sports/pop stars Optical illusions: animated clip, spinning girl Puzzle: 9 dots (on note-taking page)
Explore Analyze what a neuron with dendrites looks like. Discuss: "What areas of my brain are already dense?" Discuss: "What areas of my brain would I like to grow?" Watch video clip: "Brain Rules for Baby."	**Strategies and Tools** PPT—show ten photos of neurons Demonstrate using arms, hands, fingers Sketch a neuron with dendrites on organizer Share and discuss with process partner Record on graphic organizer (big brain) Discuss clip with group members

Extend and Expand	Strategies and Tools
Show "9 dots" puzzle—have students reflect on how they persevere. Show "lady spinning" animated clip—keep trying! Encourage each other—try various strategies. Have three students read a role-play—internal mindset voices.	"9 dots" puzzle on graphic organizer Animated clip on PPT Role-play skit Discussion of students' internal dialogue
Evaluate and Assess	**Strategies and Tools**
Have students reflect on how they developed their current mindsets. Have students brainstorm ways they could shift their mindsets.	Process partner—share Record two strategies for building a growth mindset—graphic organizer

Table 7.4 is one more sample planning guide.

Table 7.4: Planning Guide for Differentiated Instruction Using the Five Es

Lesson Title / Goal Consonant *p*	Standards
Content, Skills, and Dispositions To be able to write the letter and recognize words that begin with the consonant *p*	**Strategies and Tools** Review consonant sounds and letters that have been learned previously.
Know the Learner 50% are ELs. 30% are children of poverty. Students have a variety of learning preferences: visual, auditory, tactile, kinesthetic.	**Strategies and Tools** Tongue twisters such as "Peter Piper picked a peck of pickled peppers." Using handheld mirrors to have students watch their mouths as they say *p* words. Think-pair-share Centers
Design a Brain-Compatible Environment Multiple-modality classroom Auditory opportunities Hands-on materials Visuals and pictures	**Strategies and Tools** Seating area where children can see and hear stories and be in proximity of the teacher Centers set up with materials and space to allow students to work independently and collaboratively

continued →

Engage, Excite, Energize!	Strategies and Tools
Read stories or tongue twisters with whole group to introduce the consonant and associated sound.	Story Chart: tongue twisters
Explore	**Strategies and Tools**
Center activities ranging from simple to more complex may be assigned to specific students or selected by the students.	Work in centers to create the consonant and identify pictures and words that begin with *p*. Create the letter *p* from materials provided such as chenille, modeling clay. Cut from magazines and catalogues all the things that begin with *p*. Sort pictures that do or do not begin with *p*. Sort objects that start with *p*, *b*, *d*. Create pictures and write the word labeling them.
Extend and Expand	**Strategies and Tools**
Work with small group of students who need help recognizing the consonant, matching letters to pictures in a competitive computer program including auditory and pictorial clues. Students at a high level of readiness may be given more complex tasks of writing their own tongue twisters. Computer programs may also be provided for enrichment.	Small-group coaching Computer-assisted learning
Evaluate and Assess	**Strategies and Tools**
Assess students as they work in centers, and monitor work and understanding.	Creations in centers and discussions and observations

We hope that we will prepare students for their future and not our past. We are teaching students not for a test but for a life. When we look at the skills for the 21st century, we as educators must model those for our students. The demonstration of being a creative and critical thinker as we design curricula for our students is essential if we want all learners to stretch and grow. Solving problems and challenging situations are also necessary commodities for a successful educator. The use of data for decision making is important in the differentiation process and in being flexible and adaptable to new information. Tapping available and sometimes unavailable resources is crucial in planning for learning. Effective communication with students and colleagues helps us dig deeply to identify the needs, strengths, and preferences of our students.

We realize that educators are not transformed in a day, by reading a book or attending a conference or workshop, but through reflective practice supported by colleagues and leaders. The Teacher Self-Assessment (page 138) may be used to help focus on next steps as well as celebrate things that are already in place. To continue to grow as an educator, we believe, is everyone's goal. Changing practice may be necessary to achieve that goal and reach more learners. So set a reasonable goal, practice, reflect, and redo. It may take time, but good, deep change does. For the benefit of all—especially our students—it is truly worth it.

Children Are Like Trees

Children are very much like trees.
They differ in kind and form.
Some have grown in the open with lots of space to expand.
Others have been affected by the pressure of the forest around them.
Some have been tied to sticks to keep them straight,
While others have been allowed to develop naturally, with a minimum of pruning.
Some children are made of hard wood; others, of soft.
Like trees which may be best for shade, or fruit, or decoration,
Children have their best uses.
Some are better to look at; some are better in groups;
Others are better standing alone.
Some grow strong and sturdy; others need protection from the elements.
But every wood, every tree, and every child has a unique and different value.
We may try to graft the characteristics of a child onto another,
But we know we cannot make a palm tree into an oak or vice versa.
The best we can do is to accept the tree as it is,
To feed it, to give it light and to prune it gently to its natural shape.
And we need to remember that in working with children,
As well as in working with wood . . .
For best results, always sand with the grain.

—Author Unknown

The Art of Differentiation Is Greater Than the Sum of Its Parts

The field of differentiated instruction has grown and expanded exponentially. Some strategies are tried and true and have maintained decades of popularity and success. Newer ideas and adaptations are constantly being merged onto our best-practices list. Technology innovations have opened up another whole category of possible implementation strategies.

Understanding where and when to make adjustments and when to push and when to lighten up, designing creative projects and performances, and orchestrating powerful learning for every student are all part of the art of differentiation.

At any given time, a teacher selects multiple strategies, ideas, and tasks based on his or her personal pedagogy, a variety of data collected, and in-the-moment criteria:

- ◆ Students' readiness level and prior knowledge
- ◆ Students' general behavior and willingness
- ◆ Learning styles and intelligences profiles
- ◆ Physical classroom environment
- ◆ Instructional materials available
- ◆ Technology available
- ◆ Deadlines and required tasks
- ◆ Seasonal and weather-related circumstances
- ◆ Energy levels of teacher and students

The possibilities to think big are endless. The art of differentiation is now much greater than the sum of its parts. It still remains true that the teacher makes the difference for student learning, and becoming more precise with responsive instruction will have a real impact on student success. With the addition of a positive mindset for everyone, success for teachers and learners will follow.

Chapter Review

Eight Differentiating Characteristics of Students: A review of the characteristics of students in this digital age, *page 129*

Identifying the Attributes of Differentiation: A brief concept attainment of "yes" and "no" examples of the attributes of a differentiated classroom are charted, *page 130*

Planning Guide: A sample guide with considerations when planning for differentiated learning, *page 130*

Sample Plans: Using the planning guide, several samples are provided at different grade levels and content, *page 131*

"Children Are Like Trees" Poem: A poem is provided that will prompt discussion and reflection, *page 135*

Teacher Self-Assessment: Differentiating Curriculum and Instructional Practices: This self-assessment for teachers can provide a gap analysis for what is already happening in classrooms and what actions need to be addressed, *page 135*

Planning Guide for Differentiated Instruction

Lesson Title / Goal	Standards
Content, Skills, and Dispositions	Strategies and Tools
Know the Learner	Strategies and Tools
Design a Brain-Compatible Environment	Strategies and Tools
Engage, Excite, Energize!	Strategies and Tools
Explore	Strategies and Tools
Extend and Expand	Strategies and Tools
Evaluate and Assess	Strategies and Tools

Teacher Self-Assessment
Differentiated Curriculum and Instructional Practices

Use this self-assessment to set some personal goals and create a focus for your next steps.

Read the statements below. Mark the response that most closely describes the extent to which you use the strategy in your classroom on a regular basis.

1 = never	2 = seldom	3 = occasionally	4 = regularly

I determine the assessments I will use before I plan my unit.

    1   2   3   4

I preassess students to determine their readiness.

    1   2   3   4

I use ongoing formative assessments to guide instructional planning.

    1   2   3   4

I have the students submit an "interests" survey or self-assessment.

    1   2   3   4

I survey the students to understand their multiple intelligences profile.

    1   2   3   4

I use a variety of instructional strategies in my teaching.

    1   2   3   4

I adjust the pace of instruction to each student's needs.

    1   2   3   4

I adjust the curriculum topics to best fit my students' readiness.

    1   2   3   4

I provide a variety of resources and texts to match students' abilities.

    1   2   3   4

I provide choices in topics, processes, or products to increase motivation.

    1   2   3   4

I provide tasks and activities that reflect the multiple intelligences.

    1   2   3   4

page 1 of 2

I plan and use flexible grouping to organize students by need.

1 2 3 4

I group students by learning preferences and interests.

1 2 3 4

I have procedures and structures for a variety of activities and tasks.

1 2 3 4

I provide opportunities for movement during class time.

1 2 3 4

I prepare extension and enrichment activities for each lesson.

1 2 3 4

I encourage discussions, collaboration, and processing during tasks.

1 2 3 4

I always have an anchor activity in place for students who are finished.

1 2 3 4

I create different types of summative assessments to determine mastery.

1 2 3 4

I create rubrics to help students know assessment criteria.

1 2 3 4

References and Resources

Anderson, L., & Krathwohl, D. (Eds.). (2001). *A taxonomy for learning, teaching, and assessing: A revision of Bloom's taxonomy of educational objectives.* New York: Addison, Wesley Longman.

Aronson, E. (1978). *The jigsaw classroom.* Thousand Oaks, CA: SAGE.

Bender, W. N. (2009). *Beyond the RTI pyramid: Solutions for the first years of implementation.* Bloomington, IN: Solution Tree Press.

Bender, W. N., & Shores, C. (2007). *Response to intervention: A practical guide for every teacher.* Thousand Oaks, CA: Corwin Press.

Black, P., Harrison, C., Lee, C., Marshall, B., & Wiliam, D. (2004). Working inside the black box: Assessment for learning in the classroom. *Phi Delta Kappan, 86*(1), 9–21.

Black, P., & Wiliam, D. (2009). Developing the theory of formative assessment. *Educational Assessment, Evaluation, and Accountability, 21,* 5–31.

Blakemore, S.-J., & Frith, U. (2005). *The learning brain: Lessons for education.* Malden, MA: Blackwell.

Blakemore, S.-J., Burnett, S., & Dahl, R. (2010). The role of puberty in the developing adolescent brain. *Human Brain Mapping, 31,* 926–933.

Brain, M. (2000, April 1). *How laughter works.* Accessed at http://health.howstuffworks.com/mental-health/human-nature/other-emotions/laughter.htm on April 14, 2010.

Bridgeland, J. M., Dilulio, J. J., & Morison, K. B. (2006). *The silent epidemic: Perspectives of high school dropouts.* Washington, DC: Civic Enterprises.

Brooks, R., & Goldstein, S. (2008). The mindset of teachers capable of fostering resilience in students. *Canadian Journal of School Psychology, 23,* 114–126.

Buffum, A., Mattos, M., & Weber, C. (2009). *Pyramid response to intervention: RTI, professional learning communities, and how to respond when kids don't learn.* Bloomington, IN: Solution Tree Press.

Burmark, L. (2002). *Visual literacy: Learn to see, see to learn.* Alexandria, VA: Association for Supervision and Curriculum Development.

Caine, G., & Caine, R. N. (1997). *Education on the edge of possibility.* Alexandria, VA: Association for Supervision and Curriculum Development.

Caine, G., & Caine, R. N. (2007). *Natural learning: The basis for raising and sustaining high standards of real world performance.* Accessed at www.naturallearninginstitute.org /UPDATEDSITE/DOCUMENTS/POSITION_PAPER.pdf on May 11, 2011.

Caine, R. N., Caine, G., McClintic, C., & Klimek, K. (2005). *12 brain/mind learning principles in action.* Thousand Oaks, CA: Corwin Press.

Carvin, A. (2006, October 16). Should schools teach SMS text messaging? [Web log post]. Accessed at www.pbs.org/teachers/learning.now/2006/10/do_students_need_to _learn_text.html on May 5, 2011.

Covey, S. (1989). *The seven habits of highly effective people: Restoring the character ethic.* New York: Simon & Schuster.

Csikszentmihalyi, M. (1990). *Flow: The psychology of optimal experience.* New York: HarperCollins.

Damasio, A. (2003). *Looking for Spinoza: Joy, sorrow, and the feeling brain.* New York: Harcourt.

Damasio, A. R. (1994). *Descartes' error: Emotion, reason, and the human brain.* New York: Putnam.

de Bono, E. (1985). *Six thinking hats.* New York: Little, Brown.

Diamond, M., & Hopson, J. (1998). *Magic trees of the mind: How to nurture your child's intelligence, creativity, and healthy emotions from birth through adolescence.* New York: Penguin.

Diamond, M. C. (1967). Extensive cortical depth measurements and neuron size increases in the cortex of environmentally enriched rats. *Journal of Comparative Neurology, 131,* 357–364.

Doyle, M., & Straus, D. (1976). *How to make meetings work!* New York: Penguin.

Dunn, K., & Dunn, R. (1987). Dispelling outmoded beliefs about student learning. *Educational Leadership, 44*(6), 55–61.

Dweck, C. S. (2006). *Mindset: The new psychology of success.* New York: Random House.

Earl, L. (2003). *Assessment as learning: Using classroom assessment to maximize student learning.* Thousand Oaks, CA: Corwin Press.

Eisner, E. W. (1983). The art and craft of teaching. *Educational Leadership, 40*(4), 4–13.

Ferriter, W. M., & Garry, A. (2010). *Teaching the iGeneration: 5 easy ways to introduce essential skills with Web 2.0 tools.* Bloomington, IN: Solution Tree Press.

Fitzgerald, R. (1996). Brain-compatible teaching in a block schedule. *School Administrator, 53*(8), 20–21, 24.

Freedman, J. (2007). *The neural power of leadership: Daniel Goleman on social intelligence.* Accessed at www.6seconds.org/2007/02/27/the-neural-power-of-leadership-daniel-goleman-on -social-intelligence on July 1, 2011.

Fuster, J. M. (2003). *Cortex and mind: Unifying cognition.* New York: Oxford University Press.

Gardner, H. (1993). *Multiple intelligences: The theory in practice*. New York: Basic Books.

Gardner, H. (2006). *Multiple intelligences: New horizons in theory and practice*. New York: Basic Books.

Geake, J. G. (2009). *The brain at school: Educational neuroscience in the classroom*. New York: McGraw-Hill.

Gee, J. P. (2007). *What video games have to teach us about learning and literacy* (2nd ed.). New York: Palgrave Macmillan.

Gersten, R., Compton, D., Connor, C. M., Dimino, J., Santoro, L., Linan-Thompson, S., et al. (2009). *Assisting students struggling with reading: Response to intervention and multi-tier intervention in the primary grades* (NCEE 2009-4045). Washington, DC: National Center for Education Evaluation and Regional Assistance. Accessed at http://ies.ed.gov/ncee /wwc/publications/practiceguides/ on April 18, 2011.

Gibbs, J. (2008). *Reaching all by creating TRIBES learning communities* (30th anniversary ed.). Windsor, CA: CenterSource Systems.

Given, B. K. (2002). *Teaching to the brain's natural learning systems*. Alexandria, VA: Association for Supervision and Curriculum Development.

Goleman, D. (2006a, December 27). Aiming for the brain's sweet spot. *New York Times*. Accessed at http://opinionator.blogs.nytimes.com/2006/12/27/aiming-for-the-brains-sweet -spot/ on May 12, 2011.

Goleman, D. (2006b). Teaching to student strengths: The socially intelligent leader. *Educational Leadership, 64*(1), 76–81.

Gopnik, A., Meltzoff, A. N., & Kuhl, P. K. (1999). *The scientist in the crib: What early learning tells us about the mind*. New York: HarperCollins.

Gordon, W. J. J. (1961). *Synectics*. New York: Harper & Row.

Gregorc, A. (1982). *Inside styles: Beyond the basics*. Columbia, CT: Gregorc Associates.

Gregory, G. H. (2005). *Differentiating instruction with style: Aligning teacher and learner intelligences for maximum achievement*. Thousand Oaks, CA: Corwin Press.

Gregory, G. H. (2008). *Differentiated instructional strategies in practice: Training, implementation, and supervision* (2nd ed.). Thousand Oaks, CA: Corwin Press.

Gregory, G. H., & Chapman, C. (2007). *Differentiated instructional strategies: One size doesn't fit all* (2nd ed.). Thousand Oaks, CA: Corwin Press.

Gregory, G. H., & Herndon, L. E. (2010). *Differentiated instructional strategies for the block schedule*. Thousand Oaks, CA: Corwin Press.

Gregory, G. H., & Kuzmich, L. (2004). *Data driven differentiation in the standards-based classroom*. Thousand Oaks, CA: Corwin Press.

Gregory, G. H., & Kuzmich, L. (2005). *Differentiated literacy strategies for student growth and achievement in grades K–6.* Thousand Oaks, CA: Corwin Press.

Gregory, G. H., & Parry, T. (2006). *Designing brain-compatible learning* (Rev. ed.). Thousand Oaks, CA: Corwin Press.

Guild, P. B., & Garger, S. (1985). *Marching to different drummers.* Alexandria, VA: Association for Supervision and Curriculum Development.

Guskey, T. (2007). Using assessment to improve teaching and learning. In D. Reeves (Ed.), *Ahead of the curve: The power of assessment to transform teaching and learning* (pp. 15–29). Bloomington, IN: Solution Tree Press.

Hanniford, C. (2005). *Smart moves: Why learning is not all in your head* (2nd ed.). Salt Lake City, UT: Great River Books.

Hart, L. A. (1998). *Human brain and human learning.* Kent, WA: Books for Educators.

Hathaway, W. E., Hargreaves, J. A., Thompson, G. W., & Novitsky, D. (1992). *A study into the effects of light on children of elementary school age: A case of daylight robbery* (ERIC Document Reproduction Service No. ED343686). Edmonton, AB: Alberta Education. Accessed at www.eric.ed.gov/PDFS/ED343686.pdf on April 15, 2011.

Haynes, J.-D., Sakai, K., Rees, G., Gilbert, S., Frith, C., & Passingham, R. E. (2007). Reading hidden intention in the human brain. *Current Biology, 17,* 323–328.

Healy, J. (2010). *Different learners: Identifying, preventing, and treating your child's learning problems.* New York: Simon & Schuster.

Heuer, R. J., Jr. (1999). *Psychology of intelligence analysis.* Washington, DC: Center for the Study of Intelligence.

Hill, S., & Hancock, J. (1993). *Reading and writing communities.* Armidale, Australia: Eleanor Curtin.

Horstman, J. (2009). *The Scientific American day in the life of your brain.* San Francisco: Wiley.

Immordino-Yang, M. H., & Damasio, A. (2007). We feel, therefore we learn: The relevance of affective and social neuroscience to education. *Mind, Brain, and Education, 1*(1), 3–10.

Jarrett Thoms, K. (n.d.). *They're not just big kids: Motivating adult learners.* St. Cloud, MN: St. Cloud State University. Accessed at http://frank.mtsu.edu/~itconf/proceed01/22.html on April 18, 2011.

Johnson, D., & Johnson, R. (1991). *Cooperative learning.* Edina, MN: Interaction Book Company.

Johnson, D. W., Johnson, R. T., & Holubec, E. J. (1998). *Cooperation in the classroom.* Edina, MN: Interaction Book Company.

Kaiser Family Foundation. (2010). *Generation M²: Media in the lives of 8-12 year olds.* Menlo Park, CA: Author.

Kaplan, S., & Gould, B. (2005). *The flip book, too: More quick and easy methods for developing differentiated learning experiences.* Calabasas, CA: Educator to Educator.

Kaplan, S., Gould, B., & Siegel, V. (1995). *The flip book: A quick and easy method for developing differentiated learning experiences.* Calabasas, CA: Educator to Educator.

Kaufeldt, M. (2005). *Teachers, change your bait! Brain-compatible differentiated instruction.* Bethel, CT: Crown House.

Kaufeldt, M. (2010). *Begin with the brain: Orchestrating the learner-centered classroom* (2nd ed.). Thousand Oaks, CA: Corwin Press.

Klopfer, E. (2008). *Augmented learning: Research and design of mobile educational games.* Cambridge, MA: MIT Press.

Levine, M. D. (1990). *Keeping a head in school: A student's book about learning abilities and learning disorders.* Cambridge, MA: Educators.

Lortie, D. C. (2002). *Schoolteacher: A sociological study* (2nd ed.). Chicago: University of Chicago Press.

Lou, Y., Alorami, P. C., Spence, J. C., Paulsen, C., Chambers, B., & d'Apollonio, S. (1996). Within-class grouping: A meta-analysis. *Review of Educational Research, 66*(4), 423–458.

Louv, R. (2011). *The nature principle: Human restoration and the end of nature-deficit disorder.* Chapel Hill, NC: Algonquin Books of Chapel Hill.

Lyman, F. T. (1981). The responsive classroom discussion: The inclusion of all students. In A. Anderson (Ed.), *Mainstreaming digest* (pp. 109–113). College Park: University of Maryland Press.

Maguire, E. A., Frith, C. D., & Morris, R. G. M. (1999). The functional neuroanatomy of comprehension and memory: The importance of prior knowledge. *Brain, 122*(10), 1839–1850.

Marzano, R. J. (2007). *The art and science of teaching: A comprehensive framework for effective instruction.* Alexandria, VA: Association for Supervision and Curriculum Development.

Marzano, R. J., & Brown, J. L. (2009). *A handbook for the art and science of teaching.* Alexandria, VA: Association for Supervision and Curriculum Development.

Marzano, R. J., Pickering, D. J., & Pollock, J. E. (2001). *Classroom instruction that works: Research-based strategies for increasing student achievement.* Alexandria, VA: Association for Supervision and Curriculum Development.

Maxwell, L. E., & Evans, G. W. (n.d.). *Design of child care centers and effects of noise on young children.* Accessed at www.designshare.com/index/php/articles/chronic-noise-and-children on April 18, 2011.

Mayer, R. E. (2010). Applying the science of learning to instruction in school subjects. In R. Marzano (Ed.), *On excellence in teaching* (pp. 93–112). Bloomington, IN: Solution Tree Press.

McDaniel, C. (2003, May). *Misconceptions persist despite repeated testing.* Paper presented at the 15th annual convention of the American Psychological Society, Atlanta, GA. Accessed at www.psychologicalscience.org/cfs/program/view_submission.cfm?Abstract _ID=4095 on April 18, 2011.

Medina, J. (2008). *Brain rules: 12 principles for surviving and thriving at work, home, and school.* Seattle, WA: Pear Press.

Medina, J. (2010). *Brain rules for baby: How to raise a smart and happy child from zero to five.* Seattle, WA: Pear Press.

Meltzoff, A. N. (1999). Origins of theory of mind, cognition and communication. *Journal of Communication Disorders, 32,* 251–269.

National Research Council. (2000). *How people learn: Brain, mind, experience, and school.* Washington, DC: Author.

O'Connor, K. (2007). *A repair kit for grading: 15 fixes for broken grades.* Portland, OR: Educational Testing Service.

O'Connor, K. (2009). *How to grade for learning, K–12.* Thousand Oaks, CA: Corwin Press.

Ogle, D. M. (1986). K-W-L: A teaching model that develops active reading of expository text. *Reading Teacher, 39,* 564–570.

O'Keefe, J., & Nadel, L. (1978). *The hippocampus as a cognitive map.* Oxford, England: Clarendon Press.

Ornstein, R., & Sobel, D. (1987). *The healing brain.* New York: Simon & Schuster.

Ornstein, R., & Thompson, R. F. (1984). *The amazing brain.* Boston: Houghton Mifflin.

Panksepp, J. (1998). *Affective neuroscience: The foundations of human and animal emotions.* New York: Oxford University Press.

Pert, C. B. (1997). *Molecules of emotion: The science behind mind-body medicine.* New York: Scribner.

Posner, M., & Rothbart, M. (2007). *Educating the human brain.* Washington, DC: American Psychological Association.

Prensky, M. (2001). *Digital natives, digital immigrants.* Accessed at www.marcprensky.com/writing /prensky%20-%20digital%20natives,%20digital%20immigrants%20-%20part1.pdf on November 15, 2009.

Prensky, M. (2010). *Teaching digital natives: Partnering for real learning.* Thousand Oaks, CA: Corwin Press.

Rabin, R. C. (2010, December 20). Reading, writing, 'rithmetic and relationships [Blog post]. *New York Times.* Accessed at http://well.blogs.nytimes.com/2010/12/20/reading-writing -rithmetic-and-relationships/?scp=1&sq=reading,%20writing,%20rithmetic%20 and%20relationships&st=cse on April 18, 2011.

Ratey, J. J. (2008). *Spark: The revolutionary new science of exercise and the brain*. New York: Little, Brown.

Reeves, D. (2000). Standards are not enough: Essential transformations for school success. *NASSP Bulletin, 84*, 5–19.

Reeves, D. B. (2008). Leading to change/effective grading practices. *Educational Leadership, 65*(5), 85–87.

Reynolds, G. (2010). Phys ed: Can exercise make kids smarter? [Web log post]. *New York Times*. Accessed at http://well.blogs.nytimes.com/2010/09/15/phys-ed-can-exercise-make-kids -smarter/?emc=eta1 on May 4, 2011.

Rosenshine, B. (1997). Advances in research on instruction. In J. W. Lloyd, E. J. Kame'enui, & D. Chard (Eds.), *Issues in educating students with disabilities* (pp. 197–221). Mahwah, NJ: Lawrence Erlbaum.

Shaughnessy, R. J., Haverinen-Shaughnessy, U., Nevalainen, A., & Moschandreas, D. (2006). A preliminary study on the association between ventilation rates in classrooms and student performance. *Indoor Air, 16*(6), 465–468.

Shaw, P., Greenstein, D., Lerch, J., Clasen, L., Lenroot, R., Gogtay, N., et al. (2006). Intellectual ability and cortical development in children and adolescents. *Nature, 440*, 676–679.

Silver, H. F., & Perini, M. (2010). The 8 C's of engagement: How learning styles and instructional design increase student commitment to learning. In R. Marzano (Ed.), *On excellence in teaching* (pp. 319–344). Bloomington, IN: Solution Tree Press.

Small, G., & Vorgan, G. (2008). *iBrain: Surviving the technological alteration of the modern mind*. New York: HarperCollins.

Smilkstein, R. (2003). *We're born to learn: Using the brain's natural learning process to create today's curriculum*. Thousand Oaks, CA: Corwin Press.

Sousa, D. A. (2001). *How the brain learns* (2nd ed.). Thousand Oaks, CA: Corwin Press.

Sousa, D. A. (2006). *How the brain learns* (3rd ed.). Thousand Oaks, CA: Corwin Press.

Sousa, D. A. (Ed.). (2010). *Mind, brain, and education: Neuroscience implications for the classroom*. Bloomington, IN: Solution Tree Press.

Sousa, D. A. (2011). *What principals need to know about the basics of creating brain-compatible classrooms*. Bloomington, IN: Solution Tree Press.

Sousa, D. A., & Tomlinson, C. A. (2011). *Differentiation and the brain: How neuroscience supports the learner-friendly classroom*. Bloomington, IN: Solution Tree Press.

Squire, L., & Kandel, E. (2000). *Memory: From mind to molecules*. New York: Scientific American Library.

Stiggins, R. J. (2001). *Student-involved classroom assessment* (3rd ed.). Upper Saddle River, NJ: Merrill/Prentice Hall.

Storm, E. E., & Tecott, L. H. (2005). Social circuits: Peptidergic regulation of mammalian social behavior. *Neuron, 47,* 483–486.

Sutton, J. (2004). *Distributed models of memory.* Accessed at http://plato.stanford.edu/entries /memory/ on April 18, 2011.

Sylwester, R. (1995). *Celebration of neurons: An educator's guide to the brain.* Alexandria, VA: Association for Supervision and Curriculum Development.

Sylwester, R. (2010). *A child's brain: The need for nurture.* Thousand Oaks, CA: Corwin Press.

Szücs, D., & Goswami, U. (2007). Educational neuroscience: Defining a new discipline for the study of mental representations. *Mind, Brain, and Education, 1*(3), 114–127.

Tapscott, D. (2009). *Grown up digital: How the net generation is changing your world.* New York: McGraw-Hill.

TeacherVision. (n.d.). *Teaching students with special needs.* Accessed at www.teachervision.fen .com on April 18, 2011.

Tilton, L. (1996). *Inclusion: A fresh look—Practical strategies to help all students succeed.* Shorewood, MN: Covington Cove.

Tomlinson, C. A. (1999a). *The differentiated classroom: Responding to the needs of all learners.* Alexandria, VA: Association for Supervision and Curriculum Development.

Tomlinson, C. A. (1999b). *How to differentiate instruction in mixed-ability classrooms.* Alexandria, VA: Association for Supervision and Curriculum Development.

Tomlinson, C. A. (2010). Differentiating instruction in response to academically diverse student populations. In R. Marzano (Ed.), *On excellence in teaching* (pp. 247–270). Bloomington, IN: Solution Tree Press.

Tomlinson, C. A., & Strickland, C. A. (2005). *Differentiation in practice: A resource guide for differentiating curriculum, grades 9–12.* Alexandria, VA: Association for Supervision and Curriculum Development.

Vygotsky, L. S. (1978). *Mind in society: The development of higher psychological processes.* Cambridge, MA: Harvard University Press.

WebQuest.org. (2007). Creating WebQuests. Accessed at www.webquest.org/index-create.php on July 25, 2011.

Westerberg, T. (2009). Formative assessment: A powerful influence on teaching and learning. *Today's Catholic Teacher.* Accessed at www.catholicteacher.com/archive/articles_view .php?article_id=2131 on May 11, 2011.

Wig, G. S., Grafton, S. T., Demos, K. E., & Kelley, W. M. (2005). Reductions in neural activity underlie behavioral components of repetition priming. *Nature Neuroscience, 8,* 1228–1233.

Wiggins, G. (1993). *Assessing student performance: Exploring the purpose and limits of testing.* San Francisco: Jossey-Bass.

Wiggins, G. (1998). *Educative assessment: Designing assessments to inform and improve student performance*. San Francisco: Jossey-Bass.

Wiggins, G., & McTighe, J. (1998). *Understanding by design*. Alexandria, VA: Association for Supervision and Curriculum Development.

Williams, F. E. (1993). The cognitive-affective interaction model for enriching gifted programs. In J. S. Renzulli (Ed.), *Systems and models for developing programs for the gifted and talented* (pp. 461–484). Melbourne, Australia: Hawker Brownlow.

Willingham, D. (2009). *Why students don't like school: A cognitive scientist answers questions about how the mind works and what it means for the classroom*. San Francisco: Jossey-Bass.

Willis, J. (2006). *Research-based strategies to ignite student learning: Insights from a neurologist and classroom teacher*. Alexandria, VA: Association for Supervision and Curriculum Development.

Willis, J. (2008). *How your child learns best: Brain-friendly strategies you can use to ignite your child's learning and increase school success*. Naperville, IL: Sourcebooks.

Willis, J. (2009). *Inspiring middle school minds: Gifted, creative, & challenging*. Scottsdale, AZ: Great Potential Press.

Willis, J. (2010). Want children to "pay attention"? Make their brains curious! *Psychology Today*. Accessed at www.psychologytoday.com/blog/radical-teaching/201005/want-children -pay-attention-make-their-brains-curious on April 18, 2011.

Wolfe, P. (2001). *Brain matters: Translating research into classroom practice* (2nd ed.). Alexandria, VA: Association for Supervision and Curriculum Development.

Wolfe, P., & Sorgen, M. (1990). *Mind, memory and learning: Implications for the classroom*. Napa, CA: Authors.

Zull, J. (2002). *The art of changing the brain*. Sterling, VA: Stylus.

Index

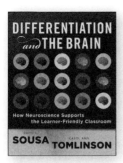

Differentiation and the Brain
How Neuroscience Supports the Learner-Friendly Classroom
By David A. Sousa and Carol Ann Tomlinson
Examine the basic principles of differentiation in light of educational neuroscience research that will help you make the most effective curricular, instructional, and assessment choices.
BKF353

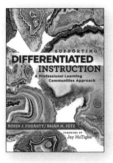

Supporting Differentiated Instruction
A Professional Learning Communities Approach
By Robin J. Fogarty and Brian M. Pete
Foreword by Jay McTighe
A practical guide to implementing differentiation in the classroom, this book offers a road map to effective teaching that responds to diverse learning needs.
BKF348

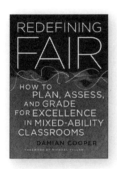

Redefining Fair
How to Plan, Assess, and Grade for Excellence in Mixed-Ability Classrooms
By Damian Cooper
Foreword by Michael Fullan
Learn how to implement equitable instruction, assessment, grading, and reporting practices to help diverse 21st century learners reach proficiency.
BKF412

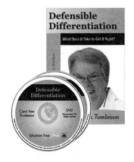

Defensible Differentiation
What Does It Take to Get It Right?
Featuring Carol Ann Tomlinson
In this keynote, Dr. Tomlinson calls on teachers to implement differentiation best practices to serve today's academically diverse student population.
72-minute DVD with presentation; CD with presentation handouts and supporting resources
DVF053

Solution Tree | Press

Wait! Your professional development journey doesn't have to end with the last pages of this book.

We realize improving student learning doesn't happen overnight. And your school or district shouldn't be left to puzzle out all the details of this process alone.

No matter where you are on the journey, we're committed to helping you get to the next stage.

Take advantage of everything from **custom workshops** to **keynote presentations** and **interactive web and video conferencing**. We can even help you develop an action plan tailored to fit your specific needs.

Let's get the conversation started.

Call **888.763.9045** today.

solution-tree.com